DATE DUE

ISO 9000 Required

ISO 9000 Required

*Your Worldwide Passport to
Customer Confidence*

Branimir Todorov

Publisher's Message by Norman Bodek

PRODUCTIVITY PRESS

PORTLAND, OREGON

© 1996 by Productivity Press, a division of Productivity, Inc.

Productivity Press
P.O. Box 13390
Portland OR 97213-0390
United States of America
Telephone: 503-235-0600
Telefax: 503-235-0909
E-mail: service@ppress.com

Cover design by Shannon Holt
Graphics by Matthew C. DeMaio
Composition by Caroline Berg Kutil
Printed and bound by Edwards Brothers in the United States of America

Library of Congress Cataloging-in-Publication Data

Todorov, Branimir.
  [ISO 9000. English]
  ISO 9000 required : your worldwide passport to customer confidence / Branimir Todorov.
    p.   cm.
  Translation of: ISO 9000: un passeport mondiale pour le management de la qualité.
  ISBN 1-56327-112-5 (hardcover)
  1. ISO 9000 Series Standards.   I. Title
TS156.6.T63   1996
658.5'62—dc20   95-46618
                                                 CIP

01   00   99   98   97   96   10   9   8   7   6   5   4   3   2   1

Contents

v

Publisher's Message

The ISO 9000 series of international quality standards is one of the most significant developments in modern quality management. The standards define the critical aspects of processes for ensuring quality in goods and services. Moreover, through auditing and certification, the standards provide a means for assuring potential customers around the world that a supplier is applying a quality system of a certain level in producing its goods or services. ISO 9000 certification is the required passport for suppliers who want to do global business today, and this book tells what you must do to qualify for it.

Much has been written about implementation of ISO 9000, from detailed handbooks to full-length works focusing on a single aspect such as documentation. Branimir Todorov's *ISO 9000 Required* fills the need for a compact and readable guide for managers to the basics of ISO. Avoiding confusing and unnecessary details, the book is a valuable primer for managers looking for a basic introduction to the

ISO management systems, as well as an accessible reference to key topics for readers already involved in ISO certification. This is an ideal book for group study with your quality and management teams. Whether your company makes goods, delivers services, or provides some combination in between, ISO 9000 *Required* will provide a common frame of reference for your team and spark their enthusiasm for ISO implementation.

Todorov begins with the basics in the first four chapters, giving a capsule history of the evolution of quality systems and explaining the primary purpose of ISO quality system certification—offering customer confidence, anywhere in the world. He tells about the quality system models, based on various standards in the series, for different types of organizations or processes. He then describes the certification process, giving advantages as well as some disadvantages, and tells about the system for accrediting the registration bodies that perform third-party certification.

In Chapter 5, Todorov turns to the relationship between the ISO 9000 standards and quality management within a company. He outlines the five basic levers of the ISO quality management system. To give readers a practical understanding of the ISO 9001 quality system (a model for quality assurance in design, development, production, installation, and servicing), Todorov sorts the standard's 20 requirements into four basic groups: leadership and people management, quality system management, process management, and management of support and improvement.

Chapter 6 takes you through guidelines and certification for service organizations, both on their own and within manufacturing operations. The basic elements of ISO 9004-2 provide the guideline for quality management in service organizations; Todorov groups these elements into six main categories for an easy-to-grasp framework.

In Chapter 7 Todorov sets out the steps involved in implementing an ISO quality system, beginning with management preparation, education, and sensitization to the need for certification and the issues involved. Management plays a critical ongoing role in the success of an ISO implementation process, and this chapter aptly describes what is required for success.

Chapter 8 focuses on the multifaceted ISO quality audit, describing it thoroughly in terms of whether it is conducted internally or by an outside agency, what the scope of the audit is, and the implementation stage at which it is carried out.

Chapter 9 presents instruments for measuring quality systems both for manufacturing companies and for service organizations. Todorov shares his easy-to-use audit questionnaires for manufacturing and service organizations, which group questions based on the requirements or basic elements of the relevant ISO standard into the main categories introduced in Chapters 5 and 6. Companies can use these valuable tools for preliminary audits, internal audits, and documentation assessments, as well as for supplier audits.

Chapter 10 addresses issues related to the cost of quality, with emphasis on how implementation of an ISO 9000 quality system can reduce the cost of nonquality. Activity-based costing is brought in as a means of tracking quality costs.

Chapter 11 focuses on changes and improvement in the 1994 revision of the ISO standards, which are captured conveniently in a table.

Chapter 12 deals with other quality standards in use today, including the QS-9000 series adopted in the mid-1990s by the Big Three automakers and their suppliers, and MIL-Q-9858A. Chapter 13 introduces the criteria developed by the Malcolm Baldrige National Quality Award, which many organizations use for internal measurement and improvement whether or not they ever apply for the award. Todorov compares the Baldrige criteria with the ISO 9004-4 guidelines for quality improvement for this purpose.

Chapter 14 talks about environmental concerns and how ISO standards implementation promotes improved environmental management. The role of the new ISO 14000 environmental standards is also discussed.

Todorov closes the book with a case study of ISO implementation at a division of Nortel in Canada, followed by a bibliography of selected articles and books related to ISO standards and quality management.

Based in Montreal, Branimir Todorov is an international quality expert who is a Quality Management Institute certified ISO 9000 auditor. This exciting book shares with a wider audience his experience-based knowledge and the assessment tools he developed while helping many different types of organizations achieve ISO certification. His insights are valuable ones, and we are pleased to be publishing his work.

We would also like to thank other individuals who made this book possible, including especially François Nadeau, who provided translation support and research assistance. Thanks also to Steven Ott, president of Productivity Press; Diane Asay, editor in chief; Karen Jones, development editing; Susan Swanson, prepress management; Aurelia Navarro, proofreading; Bill Stanton, page design; Caroline Berg Kutil, page composition; Matthew C. DeMaio, graphics composition; Shannon Holt, cover design; Joan Dickey, index.

Norman Bodek
Publisher

Quality is a lever of prosperity.

Preface

The world has changed in a spectacular fashion during the last decade and a new economic era is already in place. In this transformed business world, the ISO 9000 family of international standards for quality management has become a must for some companies, and a guide for others, in the quest for better quality and better business results. The worldwide success of these standards has led to increased interest among corporate executives as well as increased needs for training and information among managers and internal auditors; it demands an explanation of how to apply the concepts for the service economy, and requires a guide for the implementation process. In addition, many university students show an interest in quality management and in the ISO management standards. All these needs and my passion for quality moved me to write this book.

The first edition, published in French, touched its readers and sold out very quickly. In keeping with the principles of continuous improvement, I rethought suggestions from the readers, reviewed my latest experiences, and decided to write the second French and the first American edition. The book is a balance between original synthesis, interpretive figures, and professional research. It is drawn from my consulting experiences, my management seminars, interviews with practicing managers in North American and European firms, a thorough review of the professional literature, a comparative study of existing quality system standards and quality awards, university courses and numerous speeches I have given, and my training at the *Institut de Gestion Sociale* in Paris.

The goal of this book is to strengthen the competitiveness of private companies and public organizations throughout the world that use the powerful ISO 9000 tool.

The book is a practical and concise guide; it does not replace the reading and use of the standards. The ISO 9000 norms tell companies *what to do* and this book completes the instruction by telling them *how to do it*. The certification process is presented and illustrated through examples and case studies, including such well-known companies as Federal Express, Nortel, British Airways, Walt Disney, Du Pont Canada, Rhône Poulenc, Kodak Canada, Hewlett-Packard, Eurotunnel, Caterpillar, Rank Xerox, Monsanto, the automotive industry, and small businesses.

The aim of this book is to demystify the standards and to give an accurate picture of the extent, the effectiveness, and the efficiency of ISO 9000 quality systems in organizations. Beyond certification, the book's focus is on the concept and the implementation of quality systems and the way in which a company develops and supports a quality culture. A structured step-by-step implementation approach is proposed, with emphasis on leadership, empowerment, financial implications, and customization. All chapters are written with the improved ISO 9000: 1994 standards. Moreover, Chapter 6 deals with the reinvented service quality management model in depth. An original relationship between the quality tools and the requirements of the ISO 9001 standard is made to help companies in their search for implementation means.

The book presents twenty-eight original figures and twelve tables to illustrate its points. Topics include the levers of quality management, a reinvented model for service quality management supported by a 121-point ISO 9004-2 assessment questionnaire, a step-by-step implementation process, preparation of the documentation, guides for quality manuals, an internal audit diagram supported by a 126-point ISO 9001 audit questionnaire, performance measurement of the quality system, empowerment loops, quality tools, a customized cost management model, an environmental management system, quality awards models, the ISO 14000 series, the QS-9000 standards, and the advantages of the ISO 9000 system.

My analyses, syntheses, and critiques throughout the book are constructive in intent; they can clarify certain questions for companies and can serve in the future revisions of the standards.

The book is easy reading. It is meant for novices who are starting to familiarize themselves with the international standards as well as for specialists who are looking for up-to-date information and want to validate their experience with the proposed models. CEOs, presidents, managers, professors, quality and customer service coordinators, engineers, internal auditors, and students will benefit from this book. Within only 180 pages, they will find the answers to most of the questions that interest them.

Branimir Todorov

Acknowledgments

I would like to sincerely thank the people who encouraged me in the creation of this book, especially the presidents, experts, managers, professors, consultants, and students who gave me their feedback. In particular, I would like to thank my sister, Eleonora, and my mother, Elisabetha, for their encouragement; Diane Asay, Karen Jones, and Steven Ott from Productivity Press; and my assistant François Nadeau for his translation work.

I would also like to thank the International Organization for Standardization, the Standards Council of Canada, the United States National Institute of Standards and Technology, the American Society for Quality Control, the United States General Accounting Office, the European Foundation for Quality Management, the French Movement for Quality, the Quality Management Institute, Nortel, Federal Express, Xerox, Allied Signal Europe, Monsanto, Union Carbide, Hydro-Quebec, and the Business School of the University of Montreal for providing information.

ISO 9000 Required

Think locally, act globally.[1]

1

The World Market Boom

On the eve of the third millennium, as a result of revolutionary changes that have occurred around the world, we are part of an inevitable phenomenon: globalization of the economy. The world-scale expansion of markets, big and small, is a veritable boom that surpasses the bounds of ideologies, of religions, of cultural traditions, of languages or national borders, and of trade duties or regional laws. Internationalization of competition, deregulation of world trade, the boom of the information economy, and the management revolution move politicians to govern differently, presidents to manage differently, professors to teach differently, and individuals to live differently. A growing number of businesses today ask themselves, "Will we remain the same when the same is no longer fitting?"[2]

More and more companies are changing the way they do business, the way they think, and the way they manage. They are adapting to the new reality to ensure their present survival and future prosperity.

Many of them are reconfiguring their organizations and adopting new political, technical, and cultural values. Business leaders are revolutionizing their management thinking and implementing strategic information management, total quality management, empowerment, reengineering, policy deployment, cross-functional management, activity-based management, and environmental management. According to *Business Week* editor in chief Stephen Shepard, "quality may be the biggest competitive issue of the beginning of the new century."[3] Management guru Joseph Juran calls the twentieth century the Century of Productivity, and the twenty-first century the Century of Quality.[4] General Electric chief Jack Welch states, "If you can't meet a world standard of quality at the world's best price, you're not even in the game."[5]

Today, the most powerful quality initiative around the world is the set of ISO 9000 international standards for quality management. These guidelines help companies compete in the new business world. Published by the Geneva-based *International Organization for Standardization* (ISO),[6] this family of standards has known worldwide success: company by company, industry by industry, country by country, continent by continent.

In North America the first companies to adopt these international quality standards were the ones interested in the global market, business leaders such as Du Pont, Monsanto, Eastman Kodak, 3M, Hewlett-Packard, AT&T, and Nortel. The North American Free Trade Agreement (NAFTA), which expanded the North American marketplace to 380 million consumers, moved the three "amigos" to use the ISO 9000 series. In the United States, according to *Fortune* magazine, we are presently observing a genuine "isomania."[7] The American National Standards Institute has adopted the ISO 9000 series as national standard Q 9000. The United States' largest single consumer, the Department of Defense, developed the new handbook MIL-HDBK-9000 based on the international standards.[8] Federal agencies such as NASA, the Federal Aviation Administration, and the Food and Drug Administration have integrated the ISO 9000 standards into their contractual requirements.[9] Winners of the Malcolm Baldrige National Quality Award such as Xerox, Motorola, Federal Express, IBM, and others are adopting them and starting to require their suppliers to adhere to them. Finally, the Big Three automakers—Ford, Chrysler, and General Motors—have integrated the ISO 9001 and 9002 standards with their own QS-9000 standards.[10]

The Standards Council of Canada (SCC) has acted similarly, adopting the ISO 9000 standards locally as Q 9000 for the use and benefit of Canadian companies. The Canadian government has already underscored the importance of the international standards for its economy, and federal and provincial agencies are gradually introducing the ISO 9000 standards into their purchasing conditions.[11]

In Europe the European Committee for Standardization (CEN/ CENELEC) has adopted the ISO 9000 series as European standard EN ISO 9000 in replacement of each European country's national standards. In response to the creation of a common market consisting of 340 million people, and a potential market of 800 million people (European Union in 2020), the "old continent" is capitalizing on the advantages of the ISO guidelines for quality management to simplify trade. Consequently, for companies of the European Union, this series has become both a trade and a marketing tool.

The North Atlantic Treaty Organization (NATO) has also decided to replace its own quality standards. As a result, the defense departments of the sixteen members will use for their procurement the new edition of the Allied Quality Assurance Publications (AQAP) standards which are, by and large, the ISO standards.

The Pacific Rim's "tigers" (Japan, Korea, Singapore, Malaysia, Taiwan, Hong Kong, China, Australia, and New Zealand), which encompass more than two billion people, already comply to these standards.[12] As for developing countries, the international standards give them access to the European Union, to North America, and to the Pacific Rim markets. This constitutes an important factor in efforts undertaken to improve the economies of a large number of these nations.[13] Globally, companies in more than 80 countries use ISO 9000.

In an universal context, these quality guidelines improve the competitiveness of organizations. The local applicability, total universality, and global credibility of the ISO 9000 standards form a *worldwide passport for quality management* that reinforces business opportunities for companies in the new economic era.

Notes

1. John Naisbitt, *Global Paradox*, New York: Avon Books, 1995, p. 21.

2. Jean Monty, CEO of Nortel, Annual Report, 1993.

3. Stephen Shepard, "Defining the Q-word," *Business Week*, special issue 1991, p. 4.

4. Joseph Juran, "Made in U.S.A.: A Renaissance in Quality," *Harvard Business Review*, July-August 1993, p. 47.

5 Stratford Sherman, "Are You as Good as the Best in the World?" *Fortune*, December 13, 1993, p. 95.

6. ISO is the logo of the International Organization for Standardization. It is from the Greek word *isos* which means equal.

7. Ronald Henkoff, "The Hot New Seal of Quality," *Fortune*, June 28, 1993, p. 117.

8. S. A. Marash and D. Marquardt, "Quality Standards, and Free Trade," *Quality Progress*, May 1994, p. 30.

9. Cyndee Miller, "U.S. Firms Lag in Meeting Global Quality Standards," *Marketing News*, vol. 27, no. 4, February 1993, p. 1.

10. Mark Morrow, "The Steady March of ISO 9000," *Quality Digest*, May 1993, p. 22.

11. "ISO 9000 : Making Quality the Standard for Canadian Suppliers," *The Supplier*, no. 13, Spring 1993, p. 6.

12. "Where in the World Is ISO 9000?" *Quality Digest*, September 1992, p. 22-23.

13. "Les normes internationales, une clé pour l'ouverture des marchés," *ISO bulletin*, vol. 23, no. 10, October 1992, p. 3.

2
Why ISO 9000?

Quality Concept Revolution

In the beginning of the industrial era qualified artisans manufactured products under the supervision of a master and production volumes were somewhat limited. The means of ensuring quality consisted of inspecting each finished product.

At the start of this century, mass production and the evolution of technology quickly rendered unit inspection costly, ineffective, or inapplicable. This period was marked by the birth of statistical sampling for inspection and acceptance of the product at receiving and shipping. This inspection method, based on attributes that permit classification as good or bad lots, did not preclude the delivery of a certain percentage (the Average Outgoing Quality) of defective products to the buyer. In 1924 at Bell Laboratories in the United States, Walter Shewhart invented the control chart as a tool for measuring process variations.[1] In general, these statistical control methods were limited to process control and to product inspection, and served to detect non-quality.

It was only after the start of World War II that Shewhart's statistical control concepts were applied in the ZI.1-ZI.3 American war standards which were created to guarantee quality of the great number of products required for the war effort. Starting in Japan after the war, the statistical quality concept and its applications, founded on these standards, were widely taught.[2]

In the 1950s the United States introduced a new procurement concept in the military sector. Instead of gathering enough qualified inspectors to examine large quantities of goods or parts that were physically impossible to inspect, Defense Department (DoD) experts advocated quality assurance by establishing the MIL-Q-9858 standard. For the first time in history, this quality program detailed contractual specifications for procurement.[3] In the early 1960s this contractual philosophy appeared in the United Kingdom in the Polaris program in a document titled "General Requirements for the Assurance of Quality in Ships and Submarines" (GRAQs).[4]

During this period quality assurance was focused on the supplier. The idea consisted not only of inspecting parts, but of ensuring that the supplier was perfectly organized. To assure the customer, a company had to meet the following conditions: define written work methods, make sure each employee knows his or her responsibilities and possesses the required skills, identify product and process flows, and deliver good quality products. To implement this idea, purchasers, before ordering, started requiring of their suppliers a set of preventive measures and evidence of their application. However, the professional environment manifested a certain confusion between the 1950s and 1980s. The quality assurance field lacked clear distinctions and definitions of concepts such as inspection, quality control and statistical control, internal and external quality assurance, quality management, and total quality management.

Today, businesses are changing from the mass production model to the *mass customization*[5] model, and quality assurance is focused on the customer. This renewed concept consists of establishing guidelines, measures, and rules within a *quality system* that encompasses the majority of a company's activities. The key is to prevent, detect, and resolve problems of non-quality with trained employees and to demonstrate the effectiveness of the chosen measures in order to attract customer confidence. Quality assurance includes inspection and statistical quality control as a means of detection and sometimes even as a prevention tool (statistical process control). Quality management, as fine-tuned by gurus such as W. Edwards Deming, Joseph Juran, and Kaoru Ishikawa, consists in the company elaborating its own quality policy and vision for customer satisfaction. Quality management requires top-leadership commitment and a customer-focused approach that goes far beyond a service of quality assurance. In constant evolution, this concept has developed into total quality management (TQM). It integrates the employees', the customers', and the owners' satisfaction while also respecting the environment and society (see Figure 2-1).

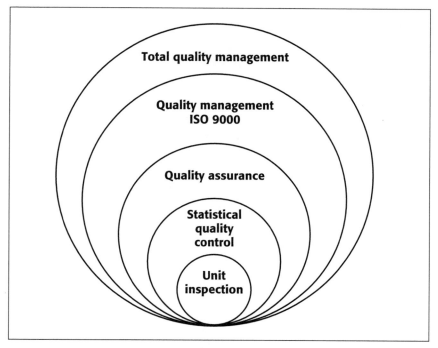

Figure 2-1. The Evolution of Quality

The ISO 9000 standards give models for quality management and quality assurance.

Why a Quality System?

Most companies are made up of owners, executives, managers, and employees in relation with customers, suppliers, and subcontractors. A company's use of a quality system promotes confidence between all these groups so as to satisfy each other's requirements. Whatever the industry and its priorities, all firms need a quality system to verify the fulfillment of their own activities and those of their suppliers and sub-contractors (the complex of goals, objectives, personnel, processes, products, services, and results), in order to win the confidence of the targeted customer in an effective and efficient manner.

Why International Standards for Quality Systems?

During the last 20 years experts have been interested in finding methods that would help buyers of goods and services have greater confidence in the quality systems of their suppliers. This phenomenon has been particularly present with big-name purchasers such as auto-makers and governments, that must be supplied with large quantities of highly dependable goods from a multitude of different suppliers. It was generally accepted that there was a need for more effective methods of ensuring product quality before delivery, instead of finding defects too late.[6]

In relations between customer and supplier, the goal of implementing a quality system is to maintain the confidence of the customer. However, if many purchasers demand different quality systems from the same supplier, the latter will not be able to implement a system that will satisfy everyone. In reality, powerful purchasers force small businesses to respect their own unique requirements before signing a contract. As a result, these companies become subject to a sizable number of external audits, wherein the auditors verify roughly the same things but according to different references. At this point, the need arises for standardization, which proposes a certain uniformity of quality assurance requirements.

Quality system standards define the contractual specifications between a purchaser and a supplier. The first standards established were the military quality programs in the United States (MIL-Q-9858) and in Canada (DND 1015-16-17). Since then NATO member countries have published the AQAP standards. Certain powerful companies and government agencies, notably the DoD, NASA, General Motors, Ford, and Chrysler, have also created standards that they have imposed on their suppliers.

Canada and the United Kingdom were the first countries to adopt national standards for quality systems (CAN3-Z299 and BS 5750). Ultimately each economic sector or country can propose its own set of norms. However, this situation risks the creation of trade obstacles (global, regional, and national) or at least trade problems; thus emerged the idea of an international standard. In the early 1980s the International Organization for Standardization (ISO) was therefore formed to establish standards for quality management and quality assurance.

The first publication was proposed in 1987 as the ISO 9000 series of international standards. Each year the ISO adds numerous other standards to clarify comprehension and utilization of the main standards in all business sectors. In 1994 the second edition of the ISO 9000 series was published, to resounding acclaim. In the view of Hitoshi Kume, an internationally recognized quality expert from Tokyo University, the extent of application of these standards is extremely broad.[7] Professor Kume finds the ISO standards very logical and notes their ability to counter weaknesses in Japanese quality management as well as help it reach higher levels.

The Utility of ISO 9000

Simplicity and confidence are crucial in the business world. In business, a company demonstrates simplicity by conforming to international standards. Thanks to such standards, a company is able to meet not only the requirements of the North American market, but also those of the Asian, Australian, European, African, and South American markets. The opening up of world trade is therefore supported by a system that ensures the smooth flow of international business. Distance and lack of information are no longer obstacles for suppliers and purchasers. Before the end of the century an intercontinental computerized network will allow businesspeople everywhere to find out, with the help of a simple query on a PC, by fax, or on the Internet, if a distant and unknown company maintains an ISO quality system.

Confidence is a logical consequence of the ISO 9000 series. Implementation of these standards should be regarded as evidence of a company's competence in attracting customer confidence. For example, thanks to ISO standards, a supplier ensures its purchaser that during design, product manufacturing, or service delivery, the supplier respected the quality procedures, isolated nonconformities, and calibrated the equipment. The ISO standards provide a starting point for trade. Without them, competition will be difficult in the global marketplace.

The ISO standards allow a company to become a world class supplier. Not so long ago supplier selection consisted of accepting the lowest bid. Today, big client companies adopt new partnership strategies with their approved suppliers. But many criteria come into play for supplier acceptance. A world class supplier must meet the requirements of the world market. The criteria most often asked for are the ISO 9000 standards, the environmental standards, electronic data interchange (EDI), and competitive prices. The new tendency adopted by large companies is to reduce the number of suppliers they use but at the same time do more business with the ones chosen.[8]

Notes

1. W. Edwards Deming, *Out of the Crisis*, Cambridge, Mass.: MIT Center for Advanced Engineering Studies, 1986.

2. Hitoshi Kume, "Le point de vue japonais sur les normes ISO 9000," *Qualité en mouvement*, no. 8, November 1992, p. 48.

3. U.S. Department of Defense, MIL-Q-9858, April 4, 1959.

4. D.G. Spickernell, "La voie vers l'ISO 9000," *ISO 9000 News*, no. 1, 1992.

5. The term is attributed to Stanley M. Davis, *Future Perfect*, Reading, Mass.: Addison-Wesley, 1987.

6. Speech given by ISO Secretary General Lawrence Eicher, New Delhi, July 1990.

7. Hitoshi Kume, "Les normes ISO 9000 at leur mise en application," *ISO Bulletin*, vol. 23, no. 8, August 1992, p. 4.

8. Danielle Luc and Branimir Todorov, "In Search of World-Class Suppliers," Montreal: Groupe de concertation sur la qualité, Montreal, September 1992.

3

What Is the ISO 9000 Family?

The ISO 9000 family is a set of 20 independent guidelines and standards for the establishment, improvement, support, and registration of quality systems. These are complementary (not alternative) to the technical product requirements. Thanks to their universality, they can be used in all business sectors. The structure of the ISO 9000 family includes the quality terminology, the principal concepts for quality, the quality system models, and guidelines for quality systems support.

The development of the ISO 9000 family is done by the ISO/TC 176 technical committee which is chaired by Canada and composed of three subcommittees and many working groups of experts. The organizational structure of this ISO technical committee is illustrated in Figure 3-1.

Quality Terminology

The ISO 9000 family is based on the quality vocabulary set forth in ISO 8402. This dictionary sets out 67 important quality terms, with definitions that result from an international consensus.

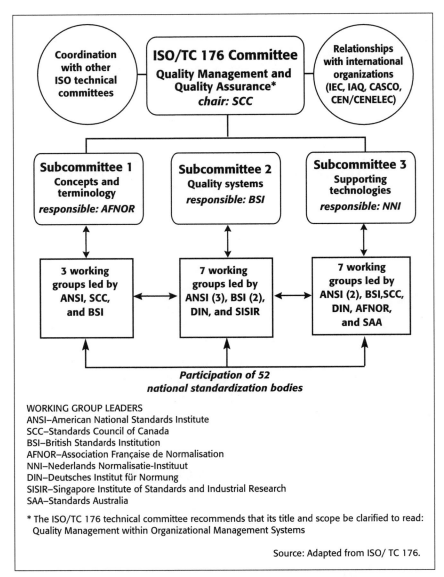

Figure 3-1. The Structure of ISO/TC 176

Quality is clearly defined by its end results: the satisfaction of stated and implied needs. *Quality management*, the heart of business management today, consists of a customer-driven policy deployed throughout the activities of a company. The *quality system* provides a fundamental means to implement quality management. It links together the organization, the quality policy, people's responsibilities, the procedures, and the processes. Finally, *total quality management* is a management approach centered on quality and aiming at a company's long-term prosperity through customer and stakeholder satisfaction as well as on the best results for the organization and society.

Quality Concepts Road Map

The ISO 9000-1 guideline is the quality concepts road map. These concepts are illustrated by the five key objectives for quality in an organization:

- quality improvement of products
- quality improvement of processes
- personnel confidence
- customer and stakeholder confidence
- fulfillment of the quality system requirements

The quality of a product has four facets: the definition of needs, the creation and design of the product, the conformity to design, and the support of the product during its useful life. All four facets must be addressed to improve product quality.

The improvement of processes involves all the company's activities. Each process is composed of inputs, value-added transformations, and outputs (results). Information flow processes are distinguished from product flow processes. The combined set of processes makes up the organization's business process network. The company must identify, analyze, manage, and continually improve its network of processes and interfaces.

Each organization, profit seeking or not-for-profit, is made up of personnel. The confidence and trust between the personnel and the executive management must be reciprocal. On one hand, executive management wants to be satisfied with the work accomplished by its employees; on the other hand, the employees want to be satisfied with their own work and career.

Each company exists due to its stakeholders: customers, personnel, owners, suppliers, and society; today's organization must satisfy the needs of each. For customers, these needs include the quality of the product; for personnel it is personal satisfaction and fulfillment; for the owners, it is the performance of their investment; for suppliers, it is sustained business; and for society it is responsible corporate citizenship.

All of these objectives are realized through a quality system linked to the network of processes and aimed at stakeholder confidence. Each quality system has an approach, a degree of deployment, and results that must be assessed periodically.

In addition to these concepts, the ISO 9000-1 guideline provides information to help companies select and use the standards for quality system models.

Quality System Models

The ISO 9000 series contains several quality system standards that should be consulted in the following order:

- ISO 9004-1: The fundamental set of elements of a quality system in a company. Intended for in-house use, this guideline provides good insight into quality management within a company and aims to obtain the required quality in an economically effective manner.
- ISO 9001: Model for quality assurance in design, development, production, installation, and servicing. This standard contains 20 quality system requirements.
- ISO 9002: Model for quality assurance in production, installation, and servicing. Suppliers ensure the manufacturing processes or service delivery. Compared with ISO 9001, this model does not include design; thus it contains 19 quality system requirements.

- ISO 9003: Model for quality assurance in final inspection and test. The supplier ensures conformity to specified requirements only for inspection and testing. Compared with ISO 9001, this model does not include design, purchasing, production, or servicing; thus it contains 16 quality system requirements.

In an universal context, the ISO models for a quality system apply to all industries or economies according to the product category market segmentation described in the next subsection.

The standards numbered from 10001 to 10020, on quality technology, constitute another category of supporting guidelines of the ISO 9000 family. These are shown in Figure 3-2. Because the standards were drawn up in different periods, there is little logic in the numbering scheme.

Scope of Application

According to Product Category

The universality of the ISO 9000 family covers all industries. Every company in the world, big or small, public or private, offers to the marketplace at least one of the four generic product categories: hardware, software, services, and processed materials (see Figure 3-3). In many cases the product is a combination of two or three categories. A computer fits into software, hardware, and services. Electricity belongs to processed materials and services. A plastic part falls between hardware and processed materials. Therefore ISO 9004-1 (hardware), ISO 9004-2 (services), ISO 9000-3 (software), and ISO 9004-3 (processed materials) standards serve as guidance.

For example, I recently conducted a feasibility study of the ISO 9000 standards within a firm of the public sector. This firm designs, produces, and installs topographic digital data files. During this project, I concluded that the product in question was part of three categories (hardware, software, and services). As a result, the suggested quality system in this case was ISO 9001, with references to the ISO 9000-3 and ISO 9004-2 standards.

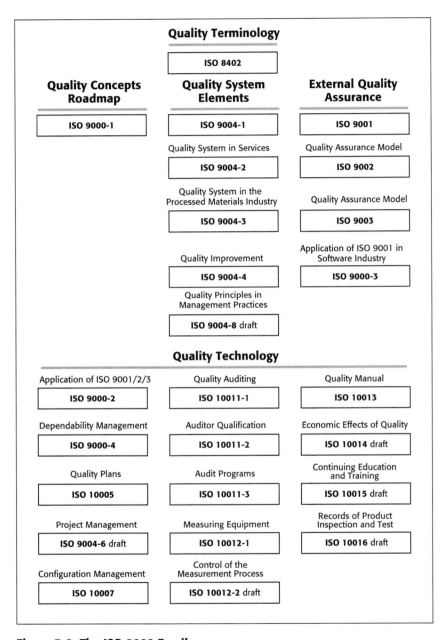

Figure 3-2. The ISO 9000 Family

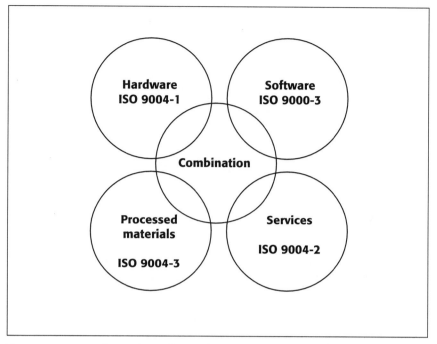

Figure 3-3. Generic Product Categories

According to Type of Process

The ISO 9000 standards serve customer needs in different types of processes. Today, companies use four ISO models for quality systems. The ISO 9001 model covers all activities from design to servicing. The ISO 9002 model ensures production, installation, and servicing. The ISO 9003 model is limited to inspection and testing. ISO 9004-2 introduces a fourth model that covers customer interface activities and service quality improvement. Figure 3-4 presents the four models for quality systems and the following examples illustrate their application.

A company that produces single-use medical syringes must have the assurance that the whole manufacturing process, from *design* to utilization, satisfies the customer requirements. This obligation reflects the characteristics of a medical product (sterilization, cleanliness). A

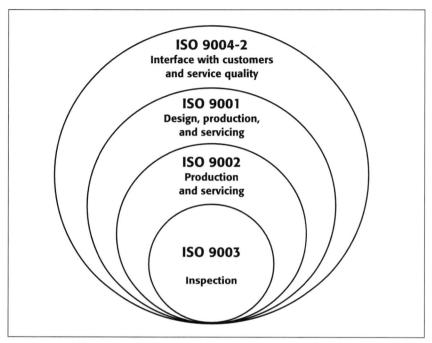

Figure 3-4. The Four Models for Quality Systems

company that manufactures gas masks for firefighters must respect all safety characteristics to protect the wearer in action. An aircraft engine manufacturer must ensure (1) the safety of the passengers and flight crew, which depends on proper functioning of the engines, and (2) the complex design process (the number of engine subsystems, the number of components in each subsystem, etc.), while respecting the proper flow of activities from design to utilization by the airlines. The standard corresponding to these three companies is therefore ISO 9001.

For a company producing plastic parts, manufacturing is the complex portion of processes. Many factors influence the parameters of the processes and the characteristics of the product (casting time, temperature, pressure, raw materials, employee training, written procedures, inspection). To prevent and detect nonconformities during *production*, the company must establish a quality system for the manufacturing processes. The corresponding standard is therefore ISO 9002.

Simple distributors need only a *final inspection* system because the design and production processes are nonexistent. Other companies having a simple manufacturing process will inspect their products only at the end of the assembly line. In both cases an inspection system is necessary and the corresponding standard is ISO 9003.

The last example concerns service companies. Bank X has several branches directly *interfacing with customers*. If there are failures during its service delivery (bad service, waiting time, slow transactions, statement errors, automatic teller machine failures) the customer will seek the same services from bank Y. To assure X's activities and service quality, the guidelines of ISO 9004-2 can be used in combination with the ISO 9001/2.

According to Quality System Situations

The different quality system situations recognized under the ISO 9000 standards system are contractual agreement between two parties, approval by the purchaser, registration by registrar, and in-house management guidance. The three ISO 9001/2/3 quality assurance models have been designed for the cases of contractual agreement, purchaser approval, and registration. For example, many government agencies require ISO 9001/2/3 models for large contracts. Companies qualify by demonstrating that their quality systems meet the requirements of these standards. Figure 3-5 lists the differences between these three models.

For in-house management guidance, the ISO 9004-1 guideline can be used. It is designed to help companies complete and improve their own quality systems and assists them in integrating it with other management systems. The approach, deployment, and results of this quality system must be maintained and improved by an assessment process. Moreover, ISO 9004-4 can be applied by companies interested in starting continuous improvement processes, implementing self-managed teams, using quality improvement tools, and improving their business results.

16 requirements

ISO 9003: 1994

1. Management responsibility
2. Quality system
3. Contract review
4. Document and data control
5. Control of customer-supplied product
6. Product identification and traceability
7. Inspection and testing
8. Control of inspection, measuring, and test equipment
9. Inspection and test status
10. Control of nonconforming product
11. Corrective action
12. Handling, storage, packaging, preservation, and delivery
13. Control of quality records
14. Internal quality audits
15. Training
16. Statistical techniques

19 requirements

ISO 9002: 1994

1. Management responsibility
2. Quality system
3. Contract review
4. Document and data control
5. **Purchasing**
6. Control of customer-supplied product
7. Product identification and traceability
8. **Process control**
9. Inspection and testing
10. Control of inspection, measuring, and test equipment
11. Inspection and test status
12. Control of nonconforming product
13. Corrective and **preventive** action
14. Handling, storage, packaging, preservation, and delivery
15. Control of quality records
16. Internal quality audits
17. Training
18. **Servicing**
19. Statistical techniques

20 requirements

ISO 9001: 1994

1. Management responsibility
2. Quality system
3. Contract review
4. **Design control**
5. Document and data control
6. Purchasing
7. Control of customer-supplied product
8. Product identification and traceability
9. Process control
10. Inspection and testing
11. Control of inspection, measuring, and test equipment
12. Inspection and test status
13. Control of nonconforming product
14. Corrective and preventive action
15. Handling, storage, packaging, preservation, and delivery
16. Control of quality records
17. Internal quality audits
18. Training
19. Servicing
20. Statistical techniques

Figure 3-5. A Comparison of the Three Quality Assurance Models

4

Certification and Accreditation

Standardization and Certification

Regulating is a matter for governments. Standardization, however, is not compulsory, but is subject to a consensus between economic partners. For example, it is not logical for a firm that produces pens for the mass market to establish a quality system according to the standards. If the pen stops writing, the consumer will buy another one without asking whether the producer complies with a norm. In this case, standardization will increase costs and will serve no purpose since it will not help obtain customer confidence. But if the same firm receives a large purchase order, over $100,000 for example, the buyer can ask for a quality system based on one of the contractual models. In such a case, the standard is a good tool that inspires confidence in the customer. Thus in the new economic era it provides a competitive advantage. But how does one prove compliance to a standard?

ISO answers this with self-audits (first party assessment) and a system of registration (also called certification). Registration can be conducted by the buyer (second-party assessment) or by a neutral outside body (third-party assessment).

In second-party registrations, customers audit their suppliers to make sure that they respect the requirements of the contractual standard; many large companies register their own suppliers. A first condition to obtaining registration consists in implementing a quality system according to the standards. The second step consists in respecting the specific requirements of the sector and product. This approach considerably diminishes the purchaser's risk of accepting a defective product. However this practice has its drawbacks. First, the resources required to evaluate and certify suppliers can be considerable when taking into account the planning and preparation of the audits as well as the frequent trips that qualified auditors must take in order to perform the on-site audits. Once these suppliers are registered it is necessary to maintain them with regular follow-up audits. When the number of suppliers becomes very high, the assessment, registration, and surveillance processes require a structured organization, appropriate means, and trained resources. Moreover, the size and clout of the supplier can become an obstacle for this type of registration. For example, when one European automaker asked to audit their tire supplier, a powerful company, the supplier merely offered to show them a brief PR video!

Third-party registration is another means of demonstrating a quality system's compliance with ISO 9001, 9002, or 9003. Following a company's request, a neutral party (a third-party registrar, also called a certification body) examines the company's quality system with respect to a chosen standard. If the results are positive, the company is certified. The quality system certificate is a company's "diploma" that indicates conformity to an international standard and provides proof of competence to gain the customer's confidence. Many companies use the certificate as a tool for working better, motivating their personnel, and obtaining independent confirmation of a quality system well implemented.

Third-party quality system registration dates to the end of the 1970s in the United Kingdom and Canada. In 1979, the Canadian Standards Association (CSA) published the Z299 standards in response to a need expressed by the major electricity suppliers and the nuclear industry. The CSA, through the Quality Management Institute (QMI), offered the only North American quality assurance registration program until 1989, when Underwriters Laboratories (UL) started alternate registration processes according to ISO 9000 standards.[1] As of 1995, 26 U.S. accredited registration bodies provide quality system certification. A list of registrars is available from RAB, NIST, ANSI, and ASQC.

In the United Kingdom, the registration process started with the British Standards Institution's (BSI) BS 5750 standards. Today the U.K. has 45,000 registered companies of all sizes and in all sectors of the economy.[2] This impressive number results from the personal prompting of former prime minister Margaret Thatcher, who encouraged British companies to obtain certification according to one of the BSI standards for better protection in the common market. As for the other European countries, the construction of the Eurotunnel spurred them to propagate quality system registration. Moreover, the English did not hesitate to ask the French for "evidence" of the quality of their work according to the British standards, since the French did not, at that time, have equivalent ones.[3]

Today the British BS 5750 standards have become the ISO 9000 series and certification is worldwide. In September, 1995, the number of ISO 9000 registered companies around the world surpasses 100,000, with the U.S. representing more than 10,000. The segmentation by country is shown in Table 4-1.

Advantages and Disadvantages of Certification

When companies aim for customer satisfaction and competitive advantage, registration becomes an important step in their quest. On one hand it instills confidence and decreases the need for external audits, which are costly for both the customer and the supplier. On

Table 4-1. ISO 9000 Worldwide Landscape

Country	Percentage of ISO 9000 registered companies*	Number of accredited registration bodies**	Accreditation body**
United Kingdom	45.0 %	42 of 48	NACCB
USA	10.5	26 of 43	RAB
Germany	6.5	21 of 21	TGA
Australia	5.5	7 of 8	JAS-ANZ
France	5.0	1 of 2	COFRAC
Netherlands	4.0	17 of 17	RvC
Italy	3.5	15 of 23	SINCERT
Japan	2.0	6 of 16	JAB
Canada	2.0	11 of 16	SCC
Belgium	1.5	11 of 11	NAC-QS
Switzerland	1.5	6 of 6	SAS
Denmark	1.5	6 of 6	DANAK
New Zealand	1.5	4 of 5	JAS-ANZ
South Africa	1.5	0 of 1	
Sweden	1.0	6 of 8	SWEDAC
Norway	1.0	5 of 5	NA
Others (60 countries)	6.5	43 of 76	18 accreditation bodies
Total	**Total**	**Total**	**Total**
76 countries	> 100,000 companies*	217 of 312 registrars	32 accreditation bodies

* Estimation done by Branimir Todorov & Associates Inc., September 1995.
** Directory of Quality System Registration Bodies, ISO Central Secretariat, third edition, 1995.

the other hand it becomes a good tool ·for employee motivation by encouraging people to attain a quality level in a tangible fashion. Most North American companies celebrate their certification by throwing a celebration event which gives the owners, senior management, customers, and suppliers a means of recognizing the employees' work through the local press, thus increasing personnel satisfaction. As one quality manager notes, it is not the American, Canadian, Asian, or European customers who read the newspaper headlines on certified companies, but rather the shop employees who are very proud to see their firm in the local press. In short, the advantages of the certification translate into both *external* (market) and *internal* (people) benefits to the company.

However, third-party certification (registration) has its disadvantages. Certain companies go through the motions only to get the ISO certificate and not to improve quality and competitiveness. This is sometimes called a "paper certificate." Since the objective is to satisfy the requirements of the registrar in the short term, this approach can easily create problems with customers in the long term. Companies that do this also run the risk of documenting, standardizing, and certifying processes, products, and services that no longer correspond to customer needs and are not competitive. Many quality experts argue that a certification based on the ISO 9000 standards is a necessary *tool* to obtain the desired results. But it will be a source of problems and will do more harm than good if it is not applied correctly. Companies must constantly bear this in mind while implementing the ISO standards.[4]

Accreditation of Certification Bodies

Two important questions that have been raised by third-party registration are the competence of registrars and the recognition of their certificates. From the beginnings of certification, registrars had full responsibility to keep their personnel competent and independent, to establish criteria for coherent assessments, and to make their certificates recognized. The dynamic evolution of this movement and the spectacular increase in the number of registrars (more than 300 in 1995) in all parts of the world have led to the creation of certain structures for the accreditation of certification bodies.

In the United States the Registrar Accreditation Board (RAB) is the organization that registers companies found certifiable through third-party assessment in accordance with the ISO 9000 series. RAB operates under the auspices of the American Society for Quality Control (ASQC) and accredits registration bodies after ascertaining their competence and reliability. An accredited registrar may then perform assessments of a quality system and certify the system to the applicable ISO 9000 series specification. When a registrar's assessors find a system certifiable, the registrar will issue a certificate to the organization and register the system in the RAB register.[5]

Canada has several registrars. To keep a certain coherence between them, the Standards Council of Canada (SCC) has established criteria and procedures for accreditation of certification bodies. Up to September, 1995, the SCC has accredited 11 registrars. According to its own criteria, the SCC will conduct annual audits of accredited registration organizations and may perform other audits at appropriate intervals to confirm adherence to the criteria and requirements for accreditation.[6] On the international level, the SCC is working to promote and support the recognition of Canadian accreditation.

In Europe, EN 45012 is the standard that supports ISO 9000 certification.[7] The standard demands a quality manual and documented procedures from the certifying agency. To ensure compliance to the 45000 series, the European Committee for Standardization (CEN) has established a new European Committee for Quality System Assessment (CES). This committee is in turn setting up a national coordinating agency in each member country of CEN. For example, the National Accreditation Council for Certification Bodies (NACCB) in the United Kingdom, the Raad voor de Certificatie (RvC) in the Netherlands, and the Trägergemeinschaft für Akkreditierung GmbH (TGA) in Germany accredit certification bodies on a national basis.

Japan, somewhat of a holdout in embracing the 9000 series given its industry's satisfaction with home-grown quality systems, is now rapidly transforming its position. There is a growing recognition in Japan of the operational benefits ISO systems can bring as well as the need for ISO registration for export sales and to coordinate assessment procedures. The Japan Accreditation Board for Quality System Registration (JAB) was created in 1993 to accredit assessment and registration bodies operating in Japan. The foundation is nonprofit and funded by the private sector.

Today the world is waiting for an international system for mutual recognition of certification. The need is obvious. Global markets have accepted the universality of the ISO standards, but they also want the same universality in certification and accreditation systems. A proposal to develop a worldwide mechanism for recognizing quality system registrations to ISO 9000 standards is being recommended for adoption by ISO and the International Electrotechnical Commission (IEC). The ISO/IEC Quality System Assessment Recognition (QSAR) program was developed and proposed by an ad hoc group formed by an ISO Council resolution. QSAR is designed to ensure that when a supplier is registered by a qualified registrar in the ISO/IEC system, the resulting registration will be recognized as valid by the supplier's customers, regardless of the location of the registrar, supplier, or customer.

The proposed recognition system is limited initially to quality system assessment and certification and to the voluntary arena. Under the proposed QSAR system, registrars accredited by qualified accreditation bodies will have complied with the technical requirements of the system and will not, therefore, require further assessment. The plan also provides a means for registrars to participate in areas not served by qualified accreditation bodies. In this situation, a registrar could apply for recognition directly to the executive office of the QSAR system. The office would, in agreement with the registrar, identify an accreditation body through which the registrar could obtain its accreditation and thereby participate in the international system. In all cases, a registrar can elect to use any qualified accreditation body.

As for the qualification of accreditation bodies, the proposed formula is a peer evaluation between them. In the views of several international experts, this system is the best mechanism that has been developed thus far. The president of RAB, George Lofgren, served on this QSAR committee and asserts that: "Based on accreditation of registrars and peer evaluation of accreditation bodies, the QSAR plan reinforces the concept of accreditation as the means of ensuring the competence of registrars and, therefore, the credibility of supplier registrations."[8] The QSAR proposal is recommended for adoption by ISO and IEC. The operation of the program will be started when at least 10 accreditation bodies of the present 32, representing every trade region of the world, will accept to participate in it, probably in the beginning of 1996.

Notes

1. Larry Rogers, "Certification du système qualité en Amérique du Nord," *Colloque: La certification des entreprises,* January 8, 1991, Paris, France.

2. Charlotte Crystal, "A Weak Commitment to Managing Quality," *International Business,* 7, no. 7, July 1994, p. 20.

3. Christian Guyard, "L'irrésistible ascension de la certification," *Industries et Techniques,* no. 724, April 10, 1992, p. 42-46.

4. Hitoshi Kume, "Le point de vue japonais sur les normes ISO 9000," *Qualité en mouvement,* no. 8, November 1992, p. 50.

5. Ronald J. Cottman, *A Guidebook to ISO 9000 and ANSI/ASQC Q90,* Milwaukee, Wisc.: ASQC Quality Press, 1993, p. 5.

6. CAN P-10, *Criteria and Procedures for Accreditation of Organizations Registering Quality Systems,* 1991.

7. EN 45012, *General criteria for certification bodies operating quality system certification.*

8. News, "ISO/IEC Mulls Over Decision to Adopt Proposal," *Quality Progress,* September 1994, p. 22.

5

The Levers of Quality Management

Quality Management

The ISO 9000 model for quality management integrates Quality Planning, Quality Control, Quality Improvement, Internal Quality Assurance, and External Quality Assurance. The first three levers are parallel to the Juran trilogy (planning, control, and improvement of quality).[1] What is new in ISO management are the Internal and External Quality Assurance.

Quality planning consists in (1) defining the firm's quality policy, (2) determining the general quality goals for the short-, medium- and long-term, and (3) specifying the quality plans and the objectives specific to the activities and to the products and services. Each business unit must create its own plan and determine its own purpose in accordance with the common goals of the company as a whole.

Quality control includes all activities and operational techniques that are used to obtain quality during all phases of the product life-cycle (for example design control, process control, and inspection) and all supporting operations (equipment control, review of noncon-forming product, and statistical techniques).

Quality improvement is a continuous cycle that starts out with the identification of nonconformities. From this preventive and corrective actions are taken to eliminate the root causes of the problems. Follow-up of the chosen actions is done through internal and external audits. The improvement cycle is completed by the management review, an analysis and assessment of feedback information (relative to the quality system and customer satisfaction) that helps management to prioritize further actions.

Internal quality assurance consists in giving management confi-dence that the targeted quality will be reached. The results of the internal audits and management reviews demonstrate the conformity, effectiveness, and efficiency of the quality system in place (respect for the quality documentation, self-inspection, inspection, quality audits, and resolution of nonconformities as well as customer complaints).

External quality assurance makes the customer confident that the requirements of the contract will be respected by the supplier. The supplier demonstrates that the functioning, maintenance, and effec-tiveness of the quality system will prevent errors in accordance with one of the contractual models (the operational and organizational pro-cedures in place and the objective evidence of their implementation).

The levers of quality management are shown in Figure 5-1.

The Demystified Quality System

Quality management operates within the quality system, indepen-dent of the product manufactured, the service offered, the software developed, or the technology utilized. To demystify the 20 require-ments of the ISO 9001 quality system, we can classify them into four groups (see Figure 5-2).

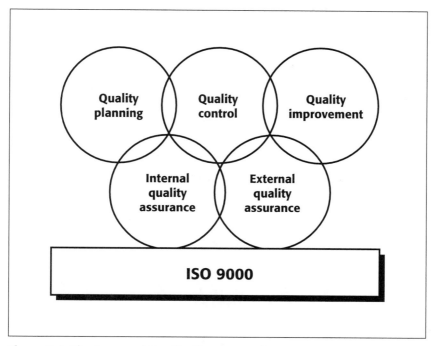

Figure 5-1. The Levers of Quality Management

I. Leadership and people management make up the first group of quality system requirements. They involve:

- the quality policy, the objectives, and the executive management commitment
- the organizational structure (the responsibilities and authorities; the means and resources to manage, to execute, and to verify work; the independence of the auditing personnel; the management representative for quality)
- the management reviews
- the internal quality audits
- the people training

Quality is no longer limited only to one department. Everyone is part of the quality system, including executive management.

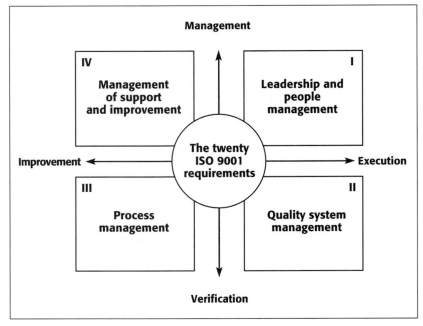

Figure 5-2. The Quality System Demystified

II. Quality system management is the second group of requirements. It concerns documentation of quality and includes:

- quality manuals, procedures, plans, and work instructions
- document and data control
- control of quality records

Establishment of the documentation provides a foundation for the
quality system; the records permit the accumulation of objective evidence.

III. Process management is the third group of requirements. It
covers the product life-cycle activities:

- contract review
- design control
- purchasing
- control of customer-supplied product

- product identification and traceability
- process control
- inspection and testing
- handling, storage, packaging, preservation, and delivery
- servicing

A complete quality system includes all quality loop activities, the phases of which are shown in Figure 5-3. All activities of the product life-cycle are harmoniously integrated in the quality system.

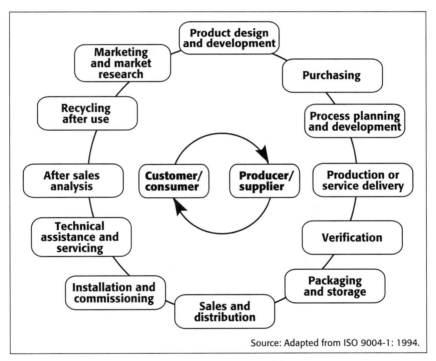

Source: Adapted from ISO 9004-1: 1994.

Figure 5-3. Product Life-Cycle Activities (the Quality Loop)

In contrast, a company that does not have a quality system has a star-shaped organizational structure in which the internal processes do not relate to each other (see Figure 5-4). This type of company has difficulty integrating incompatible activities from different business units and hits a wall in deploying its objectives.

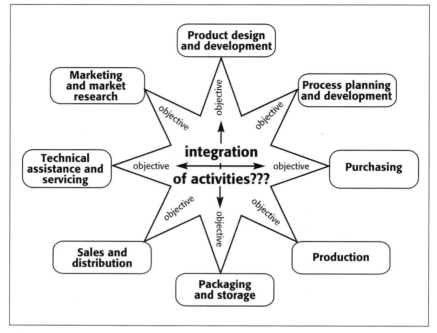

Figure 5-4. A Company without a Quality System

IV. Management of support and improvement makes up the fourth and final group:

- control of inspection, measuring, and test equipment
- inspection and test status
- control of nonconforming product
- corrective and preventive action
- statistical techniques

The quality system requires permanent support, and these activities ensure its better operation and continuous improvement.

Table 9-1 in this book provides an extensive self-assessment questionnaire for the ISO 9001 requirements, organized by the four major groups.

Notes

1. J. Juran and F. Gryna, *Juran's Quality Control Handbook*, 4th edition, New York: McGraw-Hill, 1988, p. 2.7.

6

Quality Management in the Service Economy

Trendmasters John Naisbitt and Patricia Aburdene assert that we are shifting from an industrial economy to an information (service) economy.[1] The service concept has seen radical changes in the past few years. From the passive after-sales service based on defect repair, we have now evolved to the proactive customized service which aims for customer loyalty through satisfaction of needs. Companies that achieve distinctive service often have had to redefine their very reason for doing business. Fanuc has transformed itself from an assembler of robots into a designer and installer of customized manufacturing systems. Toyota's Lexus division has invented not just a new luxury car but a whole new standard of luxury service. Taco Bell has been ringing up juicy profits because it knows that its main business is not preparing food, but delivering it.[2] Today service is a value-added product defined as "results generated by activities at the interface between the supplier and the customer and by supplier internal activities, to meet customer needs."[3] More and more service businesses ask themselves the following question: How can we improve service credibility, service quality, service effectiveness, and service efficiency to keep current customers and attract new ones?

The ISO 9004-2 guidelines help organizations introduce quality management in the service economy: tourist businesses, hospitality, medical research, health care, telecommunications, government, general trade, banking, insurance, transport, consultancy, administration, research and development, maintenance, customer services, sales and marketing, and many others. The scope of application of these guidelines is universal. Combined with the other standards of the 9000 family, ISO 9004-2 can be applied to all forms of services in the service continuum (whether solely of a service character, or in combination with the manufacture and supply of goods). The implementation of a quality system allows service organizations to manage effectively the tangible and intangible activities and interfaces.

ISO 9000 quality systems are a powerful tool for decreasing the risk of nonquality. At London's Heathrow airport, British Airways was racking up numerous complaints of lost cargo and damaged goods. While implementing ISO 9002, the company exposed the root causes of most of its problems. Managers discovered that the handlers were not trained to handle the new automated unloading equipment. After the company offered training, the operators acquired the necessary professional qualifications and are now well adapted to the technology. In the first year, thanks to ISO, complaints dropped by 65 percent and the time spent fixing problems fell by 60 percent. Audits keep BA's crew from backsliding. According to quality manager Peter Bliaux, "ISO is forcing what we should have been doing all along."[4]

The Six Facets of Quality Management in the Service Industry

The ISO 9004-2 guideline for quality management in the service economy applies for a new, modified, or existing organization. A

triangular model, illustrated in the standard, evolved from the
concept developed by Karl Albrecht.[5] It contains the key factors of a
quality system, i.e., the interaction between management responsibility, the personnel and material resources, and the structure of the
quality system. However, what is contained in the ISO management
guidelines surpasses the boundaries of a triangle. As a result of my
research, the courses I've taught, and the audits I've conducted, I
became aware that a quality system in a service company integrates six
facets of quality management (see Figure 6-1).

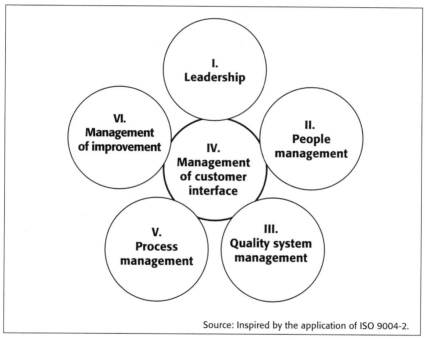

Source: Inspired by the application of ISO 9004-2.

Figure 6-1. The Six Facets of Service Quality Management

Management of the customer interface is the central facet. The
customer is the heart of the quality system. Your client is directly
linked to the service personnel and is an integral part of the service

process. Suggestions from its representatives are a driving force for improvement; it is the customer that inspires a new management style in the company.

Leadership deals with the company's quality policy as it relates to customer satisfaction, as well as with real management commitment. Executive management must clearly define the strategic goals of the services as well as the way to attain them. Also, it must implement its policy and deploy its objectives for all personnel.

People management concerns the company's human resources. It includes training, the appropriate communication, the recognition programs, personnel responsibility and empowerment, and the relationships between the employees and the customers.

Quality system management is based on documentation. The quality manual which contains the service policies and strategies, the procedures describing the processes, and the instructions that guide operations, all constitute a solid foundation for the smooth functioning of the system.

Process management covers the three principal processes of a service organization: marketing, design, and delivery. In this definition we must not forget that marketing starts with a need and delivery ends with the satisfaction of this need! The service processes are analyzed in "Customer-Defined Service Quality" on page 45.

Management of improvement is the sixth and final facet of service quality management. In fact, this element constitutes an analysis and improvement cycle made up of the following five steps:

1. Analysis of the internal assessment of the key activities and of the interfaces with customers.
2. Analysis of the customer's assessment of service quality and of data on customer satisfaction and loyalty.
3. Analysis of results from the internal quality audits and management reviews.

4. Analysis of the service performance (measurement system, comparison with the competition, benchmarking).
5. Establishment of a service quality improvement program centered on people, processes, interfaces, and results.

The analysis phases of the cycle (1 through 4) allow the service personnel to detect weak points and identify areas for improvement. The final phase (5) consists of using the results to create a service quality improvement program. Application of this program will reduce weaknesses, increase strengths, and contribute towards raising the level of the service quality.

Customer-Defined Service Quality in ISO 9004-2

The quality loop for service industries goes from the customer need for the service all the way to the analysis of the service provided (see Figure 6-2). In the loop we find service marketing, service design, and service delivery. ISO 9004-2 asks for more than a simple description of these three processes. The customer-definition of processes and interfaces is well developed and is more detailed than in the other standards of the ISO series. In service delivery, the key point is that the customer constitutes the final stage in the process. He or she is therefore the arbiter who judges the level of the service quality. If the perception is negative there is a risk of losing customers, thus the need for a quality system that prevents and detects nonquality before the service is provided. Prevention is necessary because final inspection of a service is often impossible. Repairs, rework, and rejects do not exist. Can a hairdresser modify the length of a customer's hair after cutting it too short? Can a restaurateur defuse customers' discontent if they are unhappy with their meal? Can the departure time of a plane, train, or bus be changed if the aircraft or the vehicle is late or early? Nonquality directly translates into the loss of present, faithful, and potential customers. The only real solution consists in first discerning and then avoiding nonquality. To succeed we must constantly improve the service design, or rethink and reinvent it.

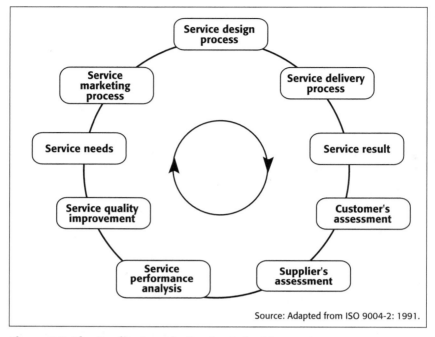

Source: Adapted from ISO 9004-2: 1991.

Figure 6-2. The Quality Loop in Service Industries

Quality Assurance in the Service Industry

Quality assurance in service organizations is concerned primarily with service design. Certain prevention and simulation methods, well known in industry, facilitate the establishment of a quality system in the services. During the design process they are very effective for avoiding potential failures in service delivery. For example, the FMECA (failure mode, effects, and criticality analysis) method estimates the level of risk of each potential failure. Three criteria come into play for this risk assessment: the probability of occurrence (the eventual frequency of the failure), the probability of nondetection (the risk of not detecting the failure if it occurs), and the severity (potential effects) for the customers. This method, created in the aeronautical industry and widely used in the automotive sector, can be applied successfully in the service design process. An example of its application for an automatic banking machine is illustrated in Figure 6-3. The first phase consists of a qualitative analysis of the potential failure (mode, cause, effect). The second phase is the quantitative analysis. It involves the assessment and reassessment of the risk and the choice of preventive actions for its reduction.

The quality system also covers the process that delivers the service. The personnel must be trained and qualified to provide excellent service to the customers. Furthermore, the firm must have adequate material resources in proper condition to ensure service performance.

In California, the Disneyland amusement park has established a quality system. Much effort was deployed to ensure the safety of visitors, to train each employee, to prevent problems, and to maintain the park with good environmental practice. To attain a high level of quality, Disneyland used the norms of the American National Standards Institute. However, Disneyland often has to deal with unique elements not foreseen by the standards. According to quality assurance superintendent Tom Corcoran, "If there isn't a standard [for an item], we develop one." Daily updates of what is happening in the park are circulated in reports titled *Facilities 1*. These reports show maintenance patterns for various attractions and help determine the causes of problems. For example, when there was a problem with a coated part at Big Thunder Mountain, the *Facilities 1* report contributed to the investigation by tracking not only descriptions of problems with the part, but also factors such as weather and attraction operating hours; the same attention is given to all details. In short, the management of Disneyland has succeeded in integrating the requirements of the existing norms and the requirements of their customers in a single standard: the Disney standard.[6] This is a key factor behind the success of this enterprise.

Certification in Service Organizations

The ISO 9004-2 standard is a guide for quality management and helps in the registration process.

Service process	Potential failure mode	Effect of failure	Cause of failure	Assessment				Preventive actions		Results			
				nondetection	occurrence	severity	risk	recommended	taken	nondetection	occurrence	severity	risk
Automatic teller (banking) machine (ATM)	ATM does not accept card	Dissatisfied customer	Card's magnetic strip	2	7	5	70	• monitor failures statistically • improve quality of magnetic strip	• improve quality of magnetic strip	2	(2)	5	20
	ATM does not return card	Very dissatisfied customer	ATM's computer control system	2	5	10	100	• improve computer control system	• improve computer control system	2	(2)	10	40
	ATM does not give correct cash	Very dissatisfied customer	A torn $20 bill	3	5	10	150	• check the bills	• use only good (verified) bills	(1)	(1)	10	10

Qualitative Analysis — **Quantitative Analysis**

Guidelines for risk assessment

$$N \times O \times S = R$$

(nondetection: 0 to 10)   (occurrence: 0 to 10)   (severity: 0 to 10)   (risk value: 0 to 1000)

Figure 6-3. FMECA Diagram for an Automatic Teller Machine

Case Example: Byrne Architects Inc.

In Halifax, Nova Scotia, the firm Byrne Architects Inc. (BAI) has been in the architectural business since 1867. BAI has established an excellent reputation for providing quality professional services in accordance with its clients' requirements. In 1994, 127 years after its founding, BAI proudly became the first architectural firm in North America to celebrate ISO 9000 certification.

BAI's attainment of ISO 9001 (ISO 9004-2) registration from registrar QMI indicates that this service company's quality policies and procedures have met the elements of this rigorous international standard. Although this registration may appear to be overambitious for a firm that does business in the Atlantic Canadian market, BAI believes that ISO 9001 is the way of the future, and in the coming years an increasing number of companies will be demanding and adopting the ISO standards to succeed in their own businesses. When these companies require architects, the Halifax firm will have its ISO registration to match its clients' standards. According to quality manager Doug Kernaghan, "We chose the highest standard in order to achieve the highest level of credibility with our clients."

It's not the first time Byrne Architects has gone out on a limb to commit to something it considers revolutionary. In 1982 BAI was one of the first firms of architects to introduce computers into their design practices at a time when few of its clients had heard of CAD. "We pioneered the use of computer graphics in Canada, and we're still advancing and upgrading our abilities." Based on its futuristic vision, this firm believes that ISO 9001 registration will become mandatory for survival by the turn of the century.[7]

Case Example: Federal Express

Federal Express is the world's largest express transportation company, providing fast and reliable services for important documents, packages, and freight. The company delivers more than two million items in 188 countries each working day, employs more than

102,000 people worldwide, and operates 464 aircraft and more than 31,000 vehicles in its integrated system. In September 1994, FedEx announced that it had received ISO 9001 registration for all of its worldwide operations.

"FedEx's ISO 9001 certification continues an important trend of quality leadership. We were the first awarded the Malcolm Baldrige National Quality Award in the service category in 1990. These accomplishments assure our customers that they are conducting business with a company that maintains high standards of quality and has processes in place to ensure internal standards," said FedEx executive vice-president William J. Razzouk. "This certification will give us a competitive advantage in the global marketplace, especially as more and more countries adopt the ISO 9000 standards. The ISO 9001 certification is an important part of increasing our business opportunities over the next decade. Specifically, it means that our customers know that FedEx will deliver what we say we're going to deliver—reliable, time-definite service backed with real-time information on their shipments."

FedEx, working with Lloyd's Register Quality Assurance (LRQA), a leading ISO 9000 registrar, pioneered a unique approach to the assessment and certification process. LRQA has conducted quality system assessments in more than 6,000 facilities on six continents. The president of LRQA asserts that "FedEx was able to use its advanced technology systems to speed up the process, save expenses, and yet still receive system-wide registration. This could not have been done without the technology that FedEx had in place."[8]

Trends

The movement toward certification of the service economy has taken root. Businesses like Federal Express and Swissair, worldwide, AT&T Customer Support and Operations, Barclays Bank Computer Operations, British Telecom, CGI (software professionals), BAI, and Nortel Business Services have already obtained ISO 9001 certification with the help of the ISO 9004-2 directives. Other companies, such as

Manpower International, Inc. with world headquarters in the United States, Apple Computer Sales & Marketing in Australia, Kodak Canada Customer Services, British Airways in Heathrow, Vodaphone Cellular in London, Meridian Hotels in Singapore, and Imperial Oil–Paramins Division in Ontario, have reached the ISO 9002 level. The use and choice of ISO 9001 or ISO 9002 combined with ISO 9004-2 varies according to the form of service, i.e., the portion of product (hardware/software) in the business processes. However, the imperative for service companies is, and will remain, quality and customer satisfaction. And certification is only a tool for improvement of credibility and quality of service organizations.

To facilitate the introduction, implementation, and improvement of a quality system in services, Table 9-2b in this book provides a 121-point questionnaire for self-assessment relative to the ISO 9004-2 norm. This questionnaire is a good tool for measuring the quality system performance of service companies.

Notes

1. John Naisbitt and Patricia Aburdene, *Megatrends 2000*, New York: Avon Books, 1991, p. 34.

2. Ronald Henkoff, "Service Is Everybody's Business," *Fortune*, June 27, 1994, p. 49.

3. ISO, *ISO 9000 Compendium*, 5th edition, 1994, p. 27.

4. Jonathan Levine, "Want EC Business? You Have Two Choices," *Business Week*, October 19, 1992, p. 58.

5. K. Albrecht and R. Zemke, *Service America!*, Homewood, Ill.: Dow Jones Irwin, 1985, p. 40-43.

6. Brad Stratton, "How Disneyland Works," *Quality Progress*, July 1991, p. 25-27.

7. "BAI First Architects in North America to Be Registered to ISO 9001," *QMI Brief*, April 1994.

8. Federal Express, "FedEx to Receive the First System-wide ISO 9001 Certification," *FedEx Fact Sheet*, September 15, 1994.

7

Step-by-Step Implementation

The establishment of a quality system in a private or public organization requires a structured approach. This includes preparation, implementation, and continuous review and support (see Figure 7-1).

Preparation

The decision to submit a company's activities to one of the ISO
standards rests with executive management. This decision can result
from internal or customer demand, from pressure of competition, or
simply from a desire to satisfy the requirements of a national or international standardization program. Much attention must be paid to the
preparation of the implementation process. It is important to answer
the following questions:

- Why?
- Where are we?
- Where do we want to go?

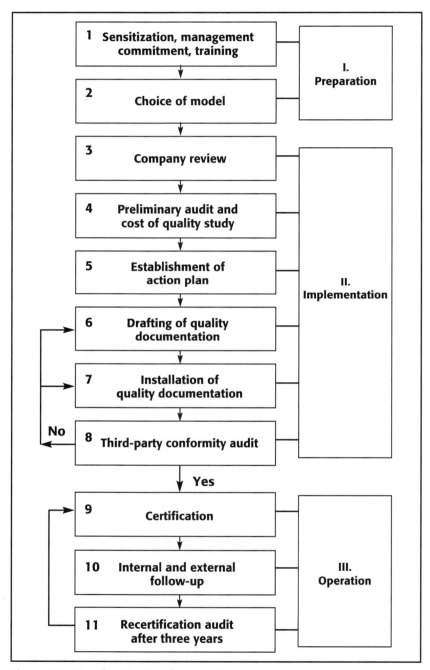

Figure 7-1. Step-by-Step Implementation

- How?
- With what means?
- With what resources?
- In what time frame?
- How much will the implementation cost?
- What will the benefits be?

Sensitization and Management Commitment

To avoid traps and to reap the full benefits of ISO 9000, executive management must play a leadership role in the implementation process. To ensure that the quality system meets the company's economic needs, it is essential that higher management fully comprehend its own role, the potential benefits of the system, the commitment necessary to implement the system, and also the resources required for implementation. Therefore management needs to form a *steering committee* and convene a brief training session so that it is sensitized to the issues just mentioned. The committee must also designate a *quality coordinator*, who is a management representative. Generally, this person is a member of the steering committee and has the necessary autonomy to execute his or her functions. This person coordinates but is not responsible for the implementation of the quality system.

The steering committee must systematically analyze the status of the quality system and the degree of staff involvement and employee motivation during its regular meetings devoted to quality. These management reviews, which are indispensable for maintaining implementation, are a powerful tool for strategic quality planning and for continuous improvement of the company. They are useful in protecting the company from bad management decisions, which can be very costly.

Information and Training

Once the decision is made, the company methodically prepares for and plans its approach. All employees must be involved, from executive management to staff and line employees. Everyone needs to understand the standards in general as well as their specific application to the activities of the organization. Various specialized courses dealing with ISO 9000 concepts and its application are available. Many companies send groups of their employees to these courses to ensure a good perception and understanding of the implementation process. To prepare for registrar BSI QA's ISO 9002 audit, Kodak Canada devoted more than 5,000 hours to train its production and procurement employees. Each one received between four and forty hours of training depending on his or her degree of participation and responsibility in the quality system.[1]

Choice of the Model

The company must choose the quality norm that best agrees with its activities. To reassure its customers and to obtain certification, a company chooses between the four models for quality systems—ISO 9001, ISO 9002 , ISO 9003, or ISO 9004-2 combined—based on nine key factors:

- Customer requirements
- Interface with customers
- Complexity of the design process
- Maturity of the design
- Complexity of the processes
- Characteristics of the product or service
- Personnel and public safety linked to the product or service
- Economic considerations
- Time for implementation (targeted)

Implementation of the Quality System

Generally the implementation of a quality system unfolds in six stages, from the company review up to certification (see Figure 7–1). The pace of implementation must be determined at the outset. An example is Hewlett-Packard (HP), which set up a worldwide certification program. In 1991, its French division started with ISO 9002 for its maintenance laboratories. In 1992, it continued ISO 9002 in its medical services and chemical analysis operations. Finally, this program continued until all entities were certified. HP's quality coordinator recognized that a company cannot do everything right away. In his opinion, it was preferable to comply to ISO 9002 in two years rather than commit to ISO 9001 in four years.[2]

In small businesses, constraints in available resources impose a gradual approach to implementation of a quality system. It is recommended to adapt the implementation process to the work pace and to the real needs for the company's evolution.

The Company Review

Before taking action the company must review its business plan, its policies and strategies for the short and longer term, and its activities. In fact, policy and process planning and validation are primordial. They are an effective means to avoid failures brought about by bad strategies or bad processes. For this type of work, competitive benchmarking is a useful tool.

The Preliminary Audit

To assess the organization's present level of quality with respect to the chosen standard's requirements, a preliminary audit must be conducted. This audit can be executed by external consultants or auditors, or by a qualified in-house quality coordinator. With the help of a prepared audit questionnaire, the lead auditor produces a synthesis report detailing the major gaps. At this stage of the implementation process a study of the costs of nonquality is also strongly recommended to support the audit findings. Methods for evaluating quality costs are analyzed in Chapter 10.

During these first steps, it is often useful to get help from an external expert for management sensitization, staff involvement, choice of model, the company review, the preliminary evaluation, the study of costs of nonquality, personnel training, creation of an action plan, cultural changes required, and any company-specific issues that arise.

The Action Plan

Identification of the gaps between the existing system and the chosen model comes out of the preliminary audit. Gap analysis helps to confirm the choice of ISO model and to identify corrective actions to be taken. The list of corrective actions forms the basis for an action plan which includes the milestones, the work groups involved, the assigned responsibilities, the resources, the estimated budget, and the target dates. Approval of this action plan by the steering committee constitutes the real startup of the ISO 9000 implementation process.

The total time span of the action plan depends on many variables, including the model used, the company's size, the internal organization, and the level of the current quality system. In practice there are companies that achieve ISO 9002 in six months and others that attain ISO 9003 in two years. In reality, the execution of the action plan is the establishment of the quality system.

Drawing Up the Quality Documentation

Document Structure and Hierarchy

The foundation of a quality system is its quality documentation, i.e., the manuals, procedures, work instructions, quality plans, and quality records. These documents correspond to three hierarchical levels of the organization—executive management, middle management, and work management—and to the product itself (see Figure 7-2).

The quality manual defines the quality policy, the quality goals and objectives, the organizational structure, and the integration of the ISO 9000 requirements. This is the policy deployment for all value-added activities of the company *(horizontal deployment)*. The quality manual also contains the documentation structure which permits the hierarchical deployment of objectives to the three levels of the firm *(vertical deployment)*. To illustrate this policy deployment, let's take the example of an airport where everyone can consult the posted "objectives," i.e., flight departure and arrival times. The pilot is responsible for transporting his or her passengers from one airport to the other at the right time; and the flight crew, both control towers, and the support personnel of both airports must work together to reach this common objective.

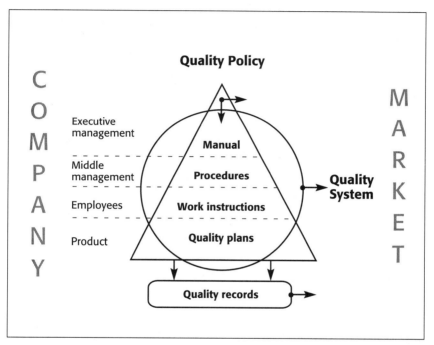

Figure 7-2. Quality System Documentation

Procedures are reference documents that explain the flow of the company's processes. For example, an airplane's takeoff encompasses the following activities: loading of the passengers' luggage, verification and preparation of the aircraft's control systems, preparation of the passengers, flight crew instructions, authorization by the control tower, and others. All these activities can be documented by one procedure.

Work instructions detail the elementary tasks and operations of each activity within the company. They help personnel do things right

the first time. Before takeoff, the pilot executes various tasks according to an instruction. Passengers follow another instruction when they secure their safety belt, and flight attendants follow still another instruction relative to their own activities.

Quality plans define the quality requirements for the products, services, or other activities. For example, the quality of the food served inflight and the quality of the airport's reception service are covered by quality plans.

Quality records are documents that preserve pertinent information of activities carried out or results obtained. The company must keep records of audit reports, management reviews, process controls, nonconformities found, preventive and corrective actions taken, personnel training courses, and other information. Like the aircraft's "black box," these records make up the company's memory and are retained for a predetermined period.

As mentioned previously, an ISO 9000 quality system was implemented for the construction yard of the Eurotunnel. The documentation principle they adopted consists in classifying design studies, equipment manufacturing, and construction into different levels of quality assurance. The goal of this classification is to distinguish between the essential and the secondary in order to reserve efforts for the essential. Taking into account the size and complexity of the Eurotunnel organization, a hierarchical documentation structure was put in place. This hierarchy allowed the affected personnel to understand their role within the system; each one used the portion that concerns him or her without having to go into the details of the whole documentation.[3]

Write Down What You Do

The ISO 9000 standards require that all work affecting quality be documented. They facilitate the organization of a company's documentation and reduce the number of useless papers. As a first step, it is important to establish the company's internal guidelines detailing the rules for documentation, i.e., the drafting, management, approval, verification, modification, and distribution of the documents. In other words, this is the document control procedure (or documentation standard). Hence, all documents must be numbered and presented in a preliminary version. Also, their contents must be approved before distribution and utilization. The steps for document write-up and control are illustrated in Figure 7-3.

Establishment of the quality documentation requires employee involvement and attribution of responsibility. The quality coordinator is responsible for the write-up of the quality manual. Tables 7-1 and 7-2 give general guidelines for the structure of a quality manual in a manufacturing and a service company. Also, the new ISO 10013 standard is a helpful tool for the development of the quality manual.

It is the responsibility of each departmental or business unit manager, not of the quality department, to lead the write-up of his or her procedures, technical specifications, and quality plans so as to manage the quality assurance for the whole unit. The manager or process engineer approves the new procedures which must then be verified by an internal quality system coordinator. The people involved in the application of a procedure must be designated in a precise manner within the procedure's responsibility section. Each procedure must contain a table of contents and a distribution list including the recipients' title and department.

Generally, a procedure contains the goals, scope, responsibilities, process flowchart and references to other documents. It answers the following questions:

- Why?
- Who does what?
- How?
- When?
- Where?

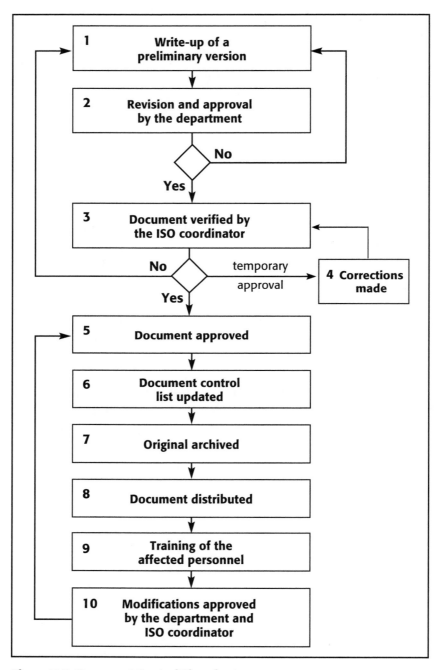

Figure 7-3. Document Control Flowchart

In practice, companies already have internal procedures in place before implementing a quality system. It is therefore necessary to compare and classify these procedures according to the chosen standard and to the new quality policy manual for revision or redesign. But for new procedures created to cover undocumented activities, the methods used by the personnel must be understood before they are put into writing. Then an independent ISO coordinator verifies that the documents satisfy the established rules and are in compliance with the chosen standard. New procedures should be complete, explicit, and in agreement with the culture of the company. Also, inclusion of a process flowchart within the procedure markedly enhances its comprehension (a sample flowchart is shown in Figure 7-4). As the old saying goes, "A picture is worth a thousand words."

One should never draw up a procedure for an unvalidated process or create a document that is difficult to understand. To ensure that a document is adequate, it is preferable that it is approved and used only after it has been validated with a practical test. Most ISO experts agree that it takes 40 hours to create a 15-page draft document. At Northern Telecom's Brampton, Ontario plant, two engineers, with the help of ten colleagues, spent five months organizing and classifying data and documents for the establishment of a quality system. The quality director declared that only the firm's long-term commitment to quality allowed them to complete the necessary documentation in five months instead of two or three years. He also noted that adequate documentation is essential for quality assurance. *"Why should people living 5,000 kilometers away believe that you sell quality products? They want proof, for example, that the measuring equipment that requires a monthly calibration has really been calibrated."*[4]

During my courses on ISO 9000 I am often asked if the existence of a large number of procedures has the effect of diminishing people's initiative and improvement suggestions. On the contrary, ISO provides a vehicle with which any employee can voice a commentary, underline a problem, or propose a solution. This mechanism is often a form that is filled out by the employee and then studied by engineers having no hierarchical link with the author. If necessary, the affected procedures are then corrected and a new version is published. The

Table 7-1. Guidelines for the Quality Manual

1. Introduction
1.1　CEO's message
1.2　Executive management commitment
1.3　Table of contents

2. Quality manual management
2.1　Manual review
2.2　Revision history
2.3　Registered holders

3. Object of the quality manual
3.1　Description of the company
3.2　Scope of the quality manual
3.3　Normative references

4. Quality system requirements (ISO 9001)
4.1　Management responsibility
　　　4.1.1 Quality policy
　　　4.1.2 Organization
　　　4.1.3 Management review
4.2　Quality system
4.3　Contract review
4.4　Design control
4.5　Document and data control
4.6　Purchasing
4.7　Control of customer-supplied product
4.8　Product identification and traceability
4.9　Process control
4.10　Inspection and testing
4.11　Control of inspection, measuring, and test equipment
4.12　Inspection and test status
4.13　Control of nonconforming product
4.14　Corrective and preventive action
4.15　Handling, storage, packaging, preservation, and delivery
4.16　Control of quality records
4.17　Internal quality audits
4.18　Training
4.19　Servicing
4.20　Statistical techniques

5. Procedures and quality plans (list or references)

6. Terms and definitions

Table 7-2. Guidelines for the Quality Manual in a Service Company

1. Introduction

    1.1   CEO's message
    1.2   Executive management commitment
    1.3   Table of contents

2. Quality manual management

    2.1   Manual review
    2.2   Revision history
    2.3   Registered holders

3. Scope of the quality manual

    3.1   Description of the company
    3.2   Scope of the quality manual
    3.3   Normative references

4. Quality system requirements (ISO 9001 + ISO 9004-2)

    4.1   Management responsibility
        4.1.1 Quality policy and customer satisfaction
        4.1.2 Organization
        4.1.3 Resources
        4.1.4 Management review
        4.1.5 Continuous improvement programs
    4.2   Quality system
    4.3   Contract review
    4.4   Service design control
    4.5   Document and data control
    4.6   Purchasing
    4.7   Control of customer-supplied product and service
    4.8   Service identification and traceability
    4.9   Service delivery process control
    4.10 Inspection and testing
    4.11 Control of inspection, measuring, and test means
    4.12 Inspection and test status
    4.13 Control of nonconforming service
    4.14 Corrective and preventive action
    4.15 Handling, storage, packaging, delivery, and protection
           of customers' possessions
    4.16 Control of quality records
    4.17 Internal quality audits
    4.18 Training
    4.19 Servicing and customer feedback
    4.20 Statistical techniques
    4.21 Interface with customers
    4.22 Service quality improvement

5. Procedures and quality plans (list or references)

6. Terms and definitions

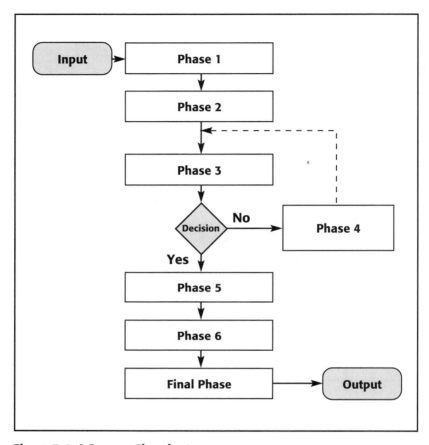

Figure 7-4. A Process Flowchart

normalized quality system does not restrain improvement and innovation; it rather favors evolution of the quality culture.

Installing the Quality Documentation

Next, you must do what you have written down. The personnel must begin to work in accordance with the new written procedures. Also the quality documentation must be tested to see if it is complete and adequate. This is a delicate exercise of linking the people with the established quality system. Figure 7-5 illustrates this practical mechanism for the implementation of a document.[5] Possible nonconformities can occur from absence of training, from documents not being under-stood clearly, or from incomplete information. Certain problems can also surface as a result of cultural resistance and old habits of the employees. It is therefore important to find time to train employees. Training must be provided each time a new document is approved.

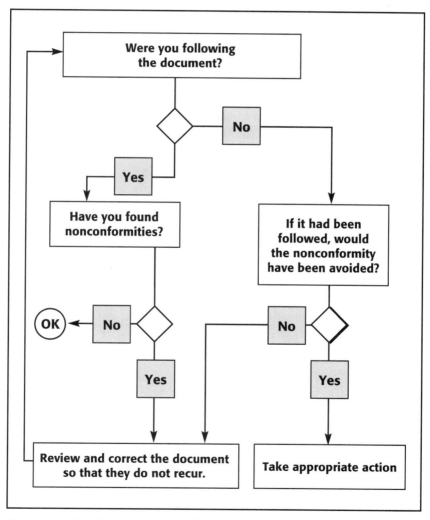

Figure 7-5. Quality Document Auditing

Documents must be configured with precision for the personnel that use them. As the standards stipulate, only the latest version of manuals, plans, and procedures can circulate within the company. Documents must be accessible to all affected personnel, at all necessary points of usage. For example, the person in charge of classifying and archiving records cannot leave on a trip without leaving the keys to his or her work site.

The executive management plays an important role in the installation of the documentation. It conducts regular management reviews to determine priorities and to ensure that the quality system is running smoothly. These reviews, based on the analysis of collected information and data, determine which business decisions to make. The quality coordinator conducts internal audits to verify and improve the implementation of documents. First and foremost, he or she must prevent or at least identify what is not working, and take actions so that it does not recur. To ensure the smoothness and effectiveness of the quality system, qualified personnel must regularly conduct internal audits. Corrective or preventive actions must be taken and followed up in order to meet the quality objectives.

Quality System Startup

Within a quality system, it is important for all people to assimilate their roles and responsibilities. Each activity must correspond to the policies of the quality manual; each department must obey the established procedures; each employee must follow the work instructions; each product must respect its plan; and, finally, each supplier must comply with the company's business processes.

The launching of the quality system represents more than a "documentation project." As the company is defining its tasks and choosing its policy, it is creating a solid knowledge base. The preparation, use, and application of the manual, procedures, work instructions, and quality plans constitute a knowledge building process.[6]

Once the quality system is running, the company can call on customers or a third-party certification body for an external audit.

Confirmation of conformity, by either of the two, represents the official startup of the quality system (see Figure 7-6).

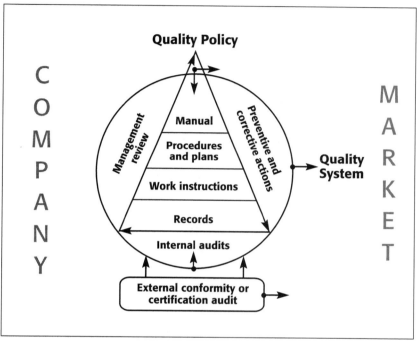

Figure 7-6. The Quality System Startup

The Third-Party Certification Process

The standards of the ISO 9000 family do not describe how to certify a company. Certification of quality systems is carried out independently by registrars according to the ISO standards, not by the International Organization for Standardization. The certification process is similar for most certification bodies; all have responsibility for their own activities. First, the company asks a registrar to certify its quality system. The registrar then supplies information regarding registration modalities: the costs, the registrar's accreditation, the steps of the certification process, and the international recognition of the certification.

After the company's request and application, the certification process contains two phases: the documentation review and the conformity audit.

The *documentation review* is an assessment by the registrar of the quality manual and procedures. The registrar verifies that the quality documentation complies with all the requirements of the standard. Following this evaluation, the company must take into account nonconformities found and put in place corrective actions to make the documentation comply with the requirements and criteria of the examining body.

As for the *conformity audit*, the registrar comes on-site to verify that the activities comply with the documentation. A team of auditors performs the audit in accordance with the ISO 10011 series. If nonconformities are raised during the audit, the registrar can give the company a time limit (according to the quantity and severity of nonconformities) to perform the necessary corrective actions. After this period has passed, the registrar returns to audit only the elements that were found noncompliant and to verify the new status of the quality system. If the audit results are positive, the registrar certifies the company's quality system according to the chosen model.

The registrar then issues the company an accreditation number, which the registrar publishes in a list the customer can consult. The certificate is valid for a predetermined period (generally three years), so long as the company respects the registrar's specific requirements relative to the conformity of the quality system.

Costs of Implementation

The global costs of the implementation process vary according to several factors: the firm's size, the complexity of the processes, the initial status of the quality system, the chosen model, and the pace of implementation. It is desirable to integrate estimation of implementation costs with establishment of the action plan (see page 58). The costs include all external resources (consultants, speakers, registrars, and auditors) and internal resources (personnel, training, equipment) involved in the implementation process. The certification costs are relatively minor when compared with the total costs of implementation. Some experts use the equivalent of person-days involved in all implementation steps to obtain a precise estimate; person-years is sometimes used for an approximate calculation. These approaches can be used in tandem to compare and confirm the estimated total costs.

Operation of the Quality System

Internal Follow-up and Empowerment

In practice, implementation of the ISO 9000 standards often represents a radical change for companies. The system must be maintained so that the company does not backslide. Old habits and work methods come creeping back very quickly as a result of lack of follow-up and support. Much as learning a new language requires constant practice, operation of a quality system requires constant maintenance.

Management reviews, systematic internal audits, and preventive and corrective actions reinforce the habits and actions of the employees. These key elements form corrective and preventive loops that are essential for the implementation and maintenance of a quality system. Management reviews and internal audits ensure that the systems are working well. Corrective actions allow the elimination of root causes of nonconformities, which is the basis for continuing improvement. Preventive actions, for their part, anticipate potential problems and initiate business process redesign. Together they avoid repetition of nonconformities, prevent occurrence of potential nonconformities, decrease costs of nonquality, and make companies more competitive.

The fact that employees have organizational freedom, responsibility, adequate training, power to resolve problems and propose corrective and preventive actions, and support from executive management, constitutes real empowerment (see Figure 7-7).

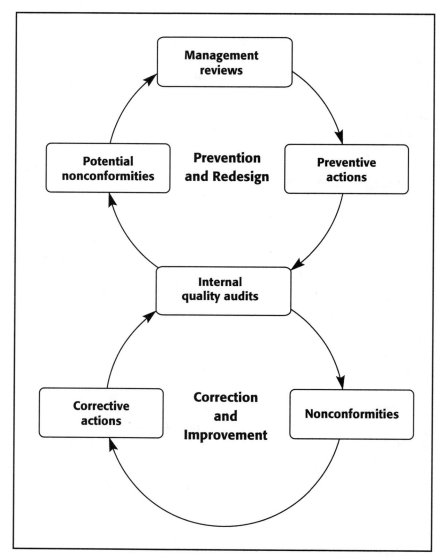

Figure 7-7. The Empowerment Loops of the ISO 9000 Standards

External Follow-up and Recertification

External audits can be conducted by customers on a regular basis. One of the goals of certification is to decrease the number of audits, which are costly to both supplier and customer. However, certification is only the first step in the implementation of a quality system, not an end in itself.

External follow-up activities begin after certification. For example QMI, a North American registrar, conducts an annual surveillance audit to make sure that a company's quality system is maintained adequately. QMI audits approximately 50 percent (ten elements) of the quality system. In the third year, at the end of the certificate's validity, QMI performs a recertification audit to renew the company's registration. This audit covers between 50 percent and 100 percent of the quality system and takes into account results of the previous audits. If the quality system is found compliant, the company receives a new three-year registration.[7] Another example is U.K. registrar BSI QA, which performs two biannual surveillance audits of 25 percent (five elements) of the system. In the United States, registration is in effect for either one or three years, depending on the complexity of the quality system. Post-registration assessments are performed every year in accordance with agreements between the registrar and the company.

Quality Tools

A wide array of quality tools can be used for the implementation of an international standard. ISO 9004-1 recommends certain ones. ISO 9004-4, for its part, proposes eleven basic tools for quality improvement. Other guides and specialized books propose a wider array of quality improvement tools. In my experience the following tools are most widely used:

- The seven basic quality tools
  - Brainstorming
  - Cause-and-effect diagram
  - Pareto chart
  - Histogram
  - Scatter diagram

    –Check sheet
    –Control charts

- The seven new quality management tools
  - Affinity diagram
  - Relations diagram
  - Tree diagram
  - Matrix diagram
  - Matrix data analysis
  - Process decision program chart
  - Arrow diagram

- Quality policy deployment (hoshin planning)
- Quality function deployment (QFD)
- Benchmarking
- Process flowcharts
- Failure mode, effects, and criticality analysis (FMECA)
- Poka-yoke (mistake-proofing)
- Fault-tree analysis
- Design of experiments (DOE or Taguchi Method)
- Statistical process control (SPC)
- Statistical sampling plan (MIL-STD-105 standards)

Table 7-3 shows the links between various quality tools and the implementation of the 20 elements of ISO 9001.

Table 7-3. Quality Tools Useful for Meeting ISO 9001 Requirements

The Quality Tools*	1. Management responsibility	2. Quality system	3. Contract review	4. Design control	5. Document and data control	6. Purchasing	7. Control of customer-supplied product	8. Product identification and traceability	9. Process control	10. Inspection and testing	11. Control of inspection, measuring, and test equipment	12. Inspection and test status	13. Control of nonconforming product	14. Corrective and preventive action	15. Handling, storage, packaging, preservation, and delivery	16. Control of quality records	17. Internal quality audits	18. Training	19. Servicing	20. Statistical techniques
Policy deployment (hoshin planning)	✓	✓																		
Quality function deployment (QFD)		✓	✓	✓					✓						✓			✓		
Failure mode, effects, and criticality analysis (FMECA)				✓		✓			✓		✓			✓	✓			✓		
Poka-yoke (mistake-proofing)									✓	✓	✓				✓			✓		
Statistical process control (SPC)									✓	✓	✓								✓	✓
Sampling plan						✓			✓											✓
Benchmarking	✓	✓		✓					✓		✓			✓	✓					
Process flowchart	✓	✓	✓	✓	✓				✓	✓	✓		✓		✓		✓		✓	
Design of experiments (DOE)			✓						✓						✓				✓	✓
The seven basic quality tools		✓			✓								✓	✓			✓	✓	✓	
The seven new quality management tools	✓												✓	✓			✓			
Fault-tree analysis (FTA)			✓						✓		✓		✓	✓	✓				✓	
Performance indicators	✓	✓	✓	✓		✓			✓		✓	✓	✓	✓			✓	✓	✓	
ISO 9001 Requirement Number	1	2	3	4	5	6	7	8	9	10	11	12	13	14	15	16	17	18	19	20

* This table presents the tools most often used according to the author's research and experience; they are not mandatory for ISO 9000 implementation.

Notes

1. "Kodak Canada," *La Presse*, Montreal, March 20, 1993.

2. Bertrand Fichou, "Dossier les normes ISO 9000," *Qualité en mouvement*, no. 4, December 1991, p. 25-34.

3. Lac Vu Hong, "Tunnel sous la Manche: La stratégie qualité," *Qualité en mouvement*, December 1991, p. 59.

4. CSA, *Focus*, special quality issue, vol. 4, no. 3, 1990, p. 3.

5. B. Todorov, "Documentation de la qualité," course notes, Paris, IGS, 1991.

6. Robert Bowen, "ISO 9000: The Foundation of a Long-Term Continuous Improvement Strategy," *ISO 9000 NEWS*, vol. 1, no. 3, May 1992, p. 10.

7. Quality Management Institute, "The QMI Registration Program," 1994.

8
Rediscovering the Quality Audit

The Power of Quality Audits

Quality audits originated from compulsory surveillance activities developed in the nuclear, space, military, and aeronautical industries. In the beginning the scope of these audits was limited to the inspection of product and process conformity with respect to a reference point. Later on, the automotive industry started practicing quality audits widely, notably for the assessment and accreditation of suppliers. At the time, the major automakers made little use of internal audits for their own structures and today they experience a lack in their management systems when it comes to internal quality assurance.

With the arrival of the ISO 9000 family and the ISO 10011 series, the quality audit has evolved to cover all facets of quality systems. Thanks to the universal applicability of these international standards, the audit has been introduced in all sectors of the economy. Thousands of enterprises of all sizes and industries have discovered the benefits of internal quality audits for improvement and upkeep of quality systems. Examples include Du Pont, Xerox, Union Carbide, British Airways, Disneyland, Nortel, Bell Canada, Motorola, IBM, Digital, Kodak, and Caterpillar, as well as the U.S. Food and Drug Administration, government agencies, and small businesses. In the new business world the quality audit is a powerful tool for quality improvement and a strong operational instrument for quality management.

The ISO standards define *audit* in the following way:

> "A systematic and independent examination to determine whether quality activities and related results comply with planned arrangements and whether these arrangements are implemented effectively and are suitable to achieve objectives."[1]

The quality system audit targets many objectives. It verifies quality system conformity, permits certification, determines the effectiveness of the quality system, offers proof of this effectiveness, and enables organizations to improve weak points and consolidate strong points. According to certain Japanese experts, the most difficult task in a company is to see anomalies. On this subject Shigeo Shingo, the renowned Japanese quality expert, relates an anecdote. While visiting a Japanese firm he saw, posted on the wall, the slogan "Eliminate Waste!" He asked the president escorting him whether all of his employees were idiots. The president, slightly taken aback, asked, "But isn't it good to get rid of waste?" Shingo pursued: "As long as someone *knows* that something constitutes waste, he will get rid of it. The big problem is not noticing that something really *is* wasteful. The slogan posted ought to be *"Find* Waste!"[2] In summary, the quality audit facilitates the discovery of nonconformities, and the latter will be potential sources for improvement.

How to Play the Game

The audit can be viewed as a game within which the actors are divided into three principal roles: the customer, the auditee, and the auditor. The ISO standards help clarify these roles. Thus, the customer requests the audit, the auditor performs it, and the auditee is examined. However, there exist several variants of the customer-auditor-auditee trio, and each participant can change its role according to the type of audit (external or internal). Concretely, the ISO 10011-1 standard provides guidelines for auditing quality systems and describes the stages to follow: initiating, preparing, performing, and reporting the audit. Auditors must be qualified according to the criteria established in the 10011-2 standard, i.e., educational background, training (including standards), assessment experience, and communication and management skills. The ISO 10011-3 standard gives advice for the management of audit programs and helps in selecting auditors for different audits.

To audit effectively, one must plan in advance and target the objectives, the scope and the purpose of the audit. The lead auditor forms a competent and trustworthy team of auditors.

During collection of evidence and interviews, the auditor must not behave like an army colonel, nor must he or she be tamed. His or her objective is to gather data, to paint a portrait of reality, and to discern facts. This is why independence of the auditor is the key factor for an effective audit. The next important characteristic of the auditor is his or her logical approach, which enables the auditor to move from elementary information to accurate conclusions about underlying causes. This approach involves a listening behavior, inductive reasoning, analogical thinking, the practice of systematic doubt, the use of analysis grids and preestablished checklists, and the art of questioning.[3]

The auditees must cooperate with the auditing team so as to contribute to adequate observations. In practice, it is difficult to perform an audit correctly without the cooperation of the auditees and a relationship based on confidence. The information received by the auditor serves to make a judgment on the effectiveness of the quality system, not on individual people.

After the audit is completed, the auditor prepares an audit report. The audit's effectiveness depends on the quality of the report, which is a synthesis of observations, conclusions, and recommendations for improvement, and which is distributed to the auditees.

Types of Quality Audits

Several types of quality audits can be distinguished according to the type of audit team, the audit's scope, and the implementation stage.

According to Type of Audit Team

Here we find two types of audits:

- The *external audit*, for which team members are external to the company (customer, purchaser, or neutral party)
- The *internal audit*, for which the team is made up strictly of company personnel

The external audit has many aims, such as the assessment and approval of suppliers; third-party certification; post-certification surveillance; and ISO 9001, ISO 9002, and ISO 9003 conformance in contractual situations.

The internal audit's objective is to examine a company's own quality system. The company president can perform such an audit to ensure that his or her policy and strategic quality goals are being attained and upkept. In practice, internal audits are often conducted by the quality coordinator, quality assurance engineers, or other qualified personnel. The usefulness of the international standards lies in their introduction and propagation of internal audits as a means for continuous improvement. Moreover, the implementation of a standard decreases the number of external customer audits. Consequently, the quality coordinator and other qualified resources can devote more of their time to internal audits. This is a great advantage for small businesses, where resources and means are often insufficient for writing up quality documentation, performing internal audits, following up corrective and preventive actions, and maintaining the quality system. Figure 8-1 details the steps of internal auditing.

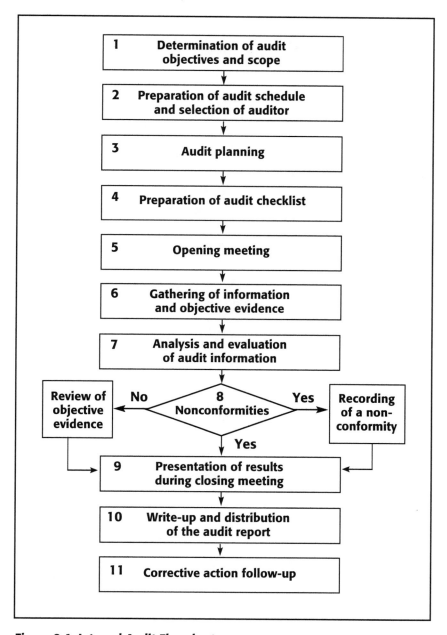

Figure 8-1. Internal Audit Flowchart

According to Audit Scope

Here we can differentiate five types of audits:

- The *system audit* is an independent assessment of the whole of the company's quality system.
- The *organization audit* deals with the resources, the responsibilities, and the interfaces of the organizational structure.
- The *process audit* applies to different activities in the process network and constitutes an independent assessment of the implementation of operational procedures.
- The *product audit* (hardware, software) is an independent assessment of the conformity of products with respect to the quality plans and technical specifications.
- The *service audit* is an independent assessment of the conformity of the service with respect to the quality plans and the service and service delivery characteristics.

According to Stage of Implementation

Here we find the following types:

- The *preliminary audit*
- The *documentation assessment*
- The *conformity audit*
- The *corrective action follow-up audit*
- The *certification audit*
- The *follow-up audit*
- The *recertification audit*

Notes

1. ISO, *ISO 9000 Compendium*, 5th edition, 1994, p. 323.

2. Shigeo Shingo, *The Sayings of Shigeo Shingo: Key Strategies for Plant Improvement*, Portland, Ore.: Productivity Press, 1987, p. 19-20.

3. Henri Mitonneau, *Réussir l'audit qualité*, Paris: AFNOR, 1988, p. 72.

9

Performance Measurement of Quality Systems

The questionnaire is the technical facet of the audit. Thanks to this analysis tool, the auditor omits no aspect of the situation and verifies all the points that were selected during the planning stage. As for the statement of questions during the interviews, this comes from the auditor's talent and communication skills.

Measurement of Manufacturing Companies

Table 9-1b (beginning on page 89) shows a proposed measurement system comprising 126 questions in reference to the elements of ISO 9001. This checklist is arranged according to the four groups of the demystified quality system (recall Figure 5-2). The first set of questions concerns leadership and people management, the second deals with management of the quality system, the third covers management of processes, and the fourth applies to management of support and improvement. The questions are formulated in an analysis grid with four possible answers: A for acceptable, IN for insufficient, UN for unacceptable and NA for not applicable. The following guidelines will help you determine what grade to assign. An answer can be considered "acceptable" if the degree of conformity is greater than 80 percent. When conformity is between 50 percent and 80 percent, the corresponding category is "insufficient." As for questions for which conformity is below 50 percent, a grade of "unacceptable" is given. The results can be synthesized for a global evaluation of the quality system's performance (P), using the following formula:

$$P = (X + 0.5Y) / (X + Y + Z)$$

where X is the number of acceptable answers, Y the number of answers that are insufficient, and Z the number of unacceptable answers.

This questionnaire can be used for preliminary audits, documentation assessments, internal audits, and supplier audits. Using it will clarify the elements of the ISO 9001 model; it is a genuine learning exercise for persons wishing to strengthen their knowledge of the international standards. Each certification body uses its own checklist, but the reference is always the standard.

Measurement of Service Organizations

Table 9-2b (beginning on page 103) shows a proposed questionnaire comprising 121 questions in reference to the elements of ISO 9004-2. This checklist is arranged according to the six facets of service quality management (recall Figure 6-1). The first set of questions concerns leadership, the second deals with people management, the third covers management of the quality system, the fourth applies to management of the interface with customers, the fifth concerns management of service processes, and the sixth deals with management of improvement. The questions are formulated in an analysis grid with the same four possible answers: A for acceptable, IN for insufficient, UN for unacceptable and NA for not applicable.

This questionnaire can be used for preliminary assessments, internal audits, and self-assessments. Its use demystifies the elements of the ISO 9004-2 model and facilitates their practical setup. It can be used as a learning exercise specifically for service companies. For certification, certain parts of this questionnaire can be used in combination with the ISO 9001 audit questionnaire. The degree of this combination depends on the type of service and on the requirements and ability of the certification body.

Table 9-1a. Correlation between ISO 9001 Requirements and Sections of the ISO 9001 Audit Questionnaire

ISO 9001: 1994 Requirements*	I. Leadership and People Management	II. Quality System Management	III. Process Management	IV. Management of Support and Improvement
4.1 Management responsibility	✓			
4.2 Quality system	✓	✓		
4.3 Contract review			✓	
4.4 Design control			✓	
4.5 Document and data control				
4.6 Purchasing			✓	
4.7 Control of customer-supplied product			✓	
4.8 Product identification and traceability			✓	
4.9 Process control			✓	
4.10 Inspection and testing			✓	
4.11 Control of inspection, measuring, and test equipment				✓
4.12 Inspection and test status				✓
4.13 Control of nonconforming product				✓
4.14 Corrective and preventive action				✓
4.15 Handling, storage, packaging, preservation, and delivery			✓	
4.16 Control of quality records		✓		
4.17 Internal quality audits	✓			✓
4.18 Training	✓			
4.19 Servicing			✓	
4.20 Statistical techniques				✓

* The element numbering is the same as in ISO 9001: 1994.

Table 9-1b. ISO 9001 Audit Questionnaire

A=acceptable	IN=insufficient	UN=unacceptable	NA=not applicable

Section I Leadership and People Management	A	IN	UN	NA	Observations and objective evidence
4.1 Management responsibility					
4.1.1 Quality policy					
1. Has executive management defined in writing (1) the quality policy, (2) the strategic objectives, and (3) its commitment to quality reflecting the mission of the company and the expectations of the customers?					
2. Has executive management communicated to all personnel (1) the quality policy, (2) the objectives, and (3) its commitment to quality?					
3. Are the quality policy and objectives understood and implemented at all levels in your organization?					
4.1.2 Organization					
4. Do the responsibilities and authorities defined in the organizational charts correspond to the in-house structure?					
5. Do the personnel who manage, perform, and verify work have the freedom and authority to:					
a. initiate preventive and corrective actions?					
b. identify and analyze any problems relating to the product, process, and quality system?					
c. recommend or propose solutions?					
d. verify the implementation of solutions?					
e. control the nonconforming product?					
6. Has your company identified the resource requirements for the managing, working, verifying, and internal auditing activities?					
7. Does your company have the trained personnel to perform the managing, working, verifying, and internal auditing activities?					

Table 9-1b. ISO 9001 Audit Questionnaire (cont'd)

A=acceptable	IN=insufficient	UN=unacceptable	NA=not applicable

Section I Leadership and People Management	A	IN	UN	NA	Observations and objective evidence
8. Are the internal auditors independent of the hierarchical structure of the audited areas?					
9. Do you have an executive management representative involved in the implementation and maintenance of the quality system?					
10. Is this person known to the company's personnel?					
4.1.3 Management review					
11. Do you examine the performance of the quality system, at regular intervals, to ensure that it is running effectively?					
12. Is the interval between management reviews defined and respected?					
13. Do you take into account audit results, preventive actions, and the level of customer satisfaction during management reviews?					
14. Do you systematically keep records of these reviews?					
4.17 Internal quality audits					
15. Do you carry out audits to determine the effectiveness of the quality sytem?					
16. Have you prepared an audit schedule? Is this schedule respected?					
17. Do you use a guide to prepare, perform, and report your audits (e.g., ISO 10011)?					
18. After an audit, do you follow up on corrective actions taken to verify their effectiveness?					
19. Have the internal audit results been brought to the attention of the personnel directly affected by these audits?					

A=acceptable	IN=insufficient		UN=unacceptable		NA=not applicable

Section I Leadership and People Management	A	IN	UN	NA	Observations and objective evidence
4.18 Training					
20. Have you identified the training needs for all people performing activities that affect quality?					
21. Are the people who perform internal audits trained?					
22. Have you identified the training needs for all people performing tasks requiring special qualification?					
23. Do you keep records of courses taken by the personnel?					
Section II Management of the Quality System					
4.2 Quality system					
24. Do you have a quality manual that describes the quality policies covering the ISO 9001 requirements, that defines the structure of the quality documentation, and that makes reference to the quality procedures?					
25. Have you established written procedures for the following activities: a. contract review?					
b. design control?					
c. documentation and data control?					
d. purchasing?					
e. control of customer-supplied product?					
f. product identification and traceability?					
g. process control?					
h. inspection and testing?					
i. control of inspection, measuring, and test equipment?					
j. inspection and test status?					

Table 9-1b. ISO 9001 Audit Questionnaire (cont'd)

A=acceptable   IN=insufficient   UN=unacceptable   NA=not applicable

Section II Management of the Quality System	A	IN	UN	NA	Observations and objective evidence
k. control of nonconforming product?					
l. corrective and preventive action?					
m. handling, storage, packaging, preservation, and delivery?					
n. control of quality records?					
o. internal quality audits?					
p. personnel training?					
q. servicing?					
r. statistical techniques?					
26. Have you established quality plans to ensure that the specified requirements of the products, projects, or contracts will be met?					
27. Do the quality plans ensure the compatibility between design, production processes, installation, servicing, and verification?					
4.5 Document and data control					
28. Have you established written procedures for the write-up, approval, distribution, update, and destruction of all quality documents?					
29. Are documents such as the quality manual, quality plans, procedures, and work instructions examined, approved, and archived before distribution?					
30. Are the appropriate documents available at all points of usage?					
31. Are obsolete documents eliminated from the points of usage?					
32. Do you have a document control list that contains the present version of all documents?					

A=acceptable	IN=insufficient	UN=unacceptable	NA=not applicable

Section II Management of the Quality System	A	IN	UN	NA	Observations and objective evidence
33. Are the people who examine modified documents the same as those who examined the preceding version?					
34. Are documents revised and approved after modifications?					
4.16 Control of Quality Records					
35. Have you established procedures for the update of quality records?					
36. Have you established procedures for the identification, collection, access, filing, and maintenance of quality records?					
37. Have you established procedures for customer access to your quality records?					
38. Do you have records for the following quality system activities:					
a. management reviews?					
b. contract reviews?					
c. design reviews, validations and verifications?					
d. subcontractors and suppliers?					
e. customer-supplied products?					
f. product identification and traceability?					
g. processes and equipment control?					
h. inspection and testing?					
i. calibration?					
j. nonconforming products?					
k. corrective actions?					
l. internal audits?					
m. training?					
n. customer information and feedback?					

Table 9-1b. ISO 9001 Audit Questionnaire (cont'd)

A=acceptable	IN=insufficient	UN=unacceptable	NA=not applicable

Section II Management of the Quality System	A	IN	UN	NA	Observations and objective evidence
39. Are quality records maintained for an agreed-to period?					
40. Are quality records readily retrievable?					
Section III Management of Processes					
4.3 Contract review					
41. Do you verify the tender before submission, and the contract or order before acceptance, to ensure that the requirements are adequately defined and documented?					
42. Do you verify that all differences between the order requirements and those in the tender are resolved?					
43. During contract reviews, do you verify your capacity to meet the customer's statement of requirements?					
44. Do you keep records of these reviews?					
4.4 Design control					
45. Have you defined the responsibilities, roles, and means of the people and departments participating in the stages of the design process?					
46. Are the interfaces between these participants defined?					
47. Do you plan all stages of design?					
48. Are (1) verification and (2) validation activities performed throughout all stages of design?					
49. Are reviews of critical product characteristics performed at the end of each stage of design?					
50. Are design modifications controlled (configuration management)?					

A=acceptable	IN=insufficient			UN=unacceptable	NA=not applicable

Section III Management of Processes	A	IN	UN	NA	Observations and objective evidence
4.6 Purchasing					
51. Do you assess and select suppliers and subcontractors on the basis of quality assurance requirements of (1) the product and (2) the system?					
52. Are purchasing order data verified before being sent to suppliers and subcontractors?					
53. Are purchased products verified in conformance with preestablished procedures?					
4.7 Control of customer-supplied product					
54. When a customer provides a product (raw material, part, equipment, service, software), do you verify, store, and maintain the customer-supplied product according to established procedures?					
55. Do you inform the customer in the case of nonconformities in the supplied product? Do you keep records and reports of these nonconformities?					
4.8 Product identification and traceability					
56. Are products identified throughout the whole product life cycle?					
57. Is the product identification, by unit or by lot, reliable?					
58. Does the product identification respect the preestablished procedure?					
59. Do you keep records of product identification and traceability according to customer contractual requirements?					
4.9 Process control					
60. Are the processes, from production to servicing, planned and documented?					

Table 9-1b. ISO 9001 Audit Questionnaire (cont'd)

| A=acceptable | IN=insufficient | UN=unacceptable | NA=not applicable |

Section III Management of Processes	A	IN	UN	NA	Observations and objective evidence
61. Before starting a new production process, do you perform a capability study and/or obtain approval for the processes involved?					
62. Are the procedures for process control respected (process parameters and product characteristics)?					
63. Are the procedures for control of maintenance equipment for production, installation, and servicing respected?					
64. Do you clearly define the criteria for workmanship (quality plans, tolerance intervals, samples, standards, specific requirements)?					
65. Are the procedures for control of nonverifiable processes respected?					
66. Do you have the qualified personnel and the appropriate equipment to perform nonverifiable processes?					
67. Do you have a recall system for products that are released (without verification) for urgent production purposes?					
68. Before starting a new process, do you prepare documented procedures?					
69. Do you approve processes, equipment, and the work environment as appropriate?					
70. Do you keep records for: (1) process capability, (2) equipment used, and (3) affected personnel?					
4.10 Inspection and testing					
71. Do you perform receiving inspection according to procedures or quality plans?					
72. Do you perform in-process inspection and/or self-inspection according to procedures or quality plans?					

A=acceptable	IN=insufficient	UN=unacceptable	NA=not applicable

Section III Management of Processes	A	IN	UN	NA	Observations and objective evidence
73. Are finished products inspected and tested in accordance with quality procedures and/or quality plans?					
74. Do you verify, before shipping, that all planned inspections and tests have been performed and that the results are acceptable?					
75. Do you keep records proving that the product has been inspected and/or tested?					
4.15 Handling, storage, packaging, preservation, and delivery					
76. Do you have procedures for handling and are they followed?					
77. Do you have procedures for storage and are they respected?					
78. Are the procedures for disposition of nonconforming products during the storage and delivery activities implemented?					
79. Do you have procedures covering the activities of packaging and preservation, and are they followed?					
80. Do you have procedures concerning delivery, and are they respected?					
4.19 Servicing					
81. Do you have a procedure for servicing and is it respected when servicing is a contractual requirement?					
82. Does this procedure result from a study of customer expectations and needs?					
83. Do you have a system for the analysis of customer feedback?					
84. Is immediate replacement possible for products sold under warranty?					

Table 9-1b. ISO 9001 Audit Questionnaire (cont'd)

A=acceptable	IN=insufficient	UN=unacceptable	NA=not applicable

Section III Management of Processes	A	IN	UN	NA	Observations and objective evidence
85. Do you have a procedure for disposition of repairs, and is it followed?					
86. Do you supply assistance for customer training and installation of the product?					
87. Does a customer documentation package exist for maintenance and usage of the sold product, and is it adequate?					
88. Are you committed to providing replacement parts?					
Section IV Management of Support and Improvement					
4.11 Control of inspection, measuring, and test equipment					
89. Does the inspection, measuring, and test equipment ensure that the measurement uncertainty is consistent with the required measurement capability?					
90. Are all inspections and measurements made with specifically identified equipment?					
91. Are all inspections and measurements made with adjusted equipment?					
92. Are all inspections and measurements made with calibrated equipment?					
93. Are inspection, measuring, and test equipment and test software controlled and maintained in accordance with a documented procedure?					
94. Do you keep records of the calibration of inspection, measuring, and test equipment?					
95. Have you used a reference standard (e.g. ISO 10012) for the control of inspection, measuring, and test equipment?					

A=acceptable	IN=insufficient	UN=unacceptable	NA=not applicable

Section IV Management of Support and Improvement	A	IN	UN	NA	Observations and objective evidence
96. Do you identify the calibration status of inspection, measuring, and test equipment with a suitable indicator?					
97. When no nationally or internationally recognized standards exist, is the basis used for calibration documented?					
4.12 Inspection and test status					
98. Do you indicate *conformance* of the product with suitable means, in accordance with procedures or quality plans?					
99. Do you indicate *nonconformance* of the product with suitable means, in accordance with procedures or quality plans?					
100. Do you know, at all times, the status of the *planned* inspections and tests and the results of the inspections and tests that have been *performed?*					
4.13 Control of nonconforming product					
101. Are nonconforming products identified according to a procedure?					
102. Are nonconforming products isolated according to a procedure?					
103. Are nonconforming products reviewed in accordance with a procedure?					
104. Do you have procedures for disposition of nonconforming products: a. in rework cases?					
b. in cases of acceptance by concession?					
c. in cases of regrading for alternative applications?					
d. in cases of rejection or scrapping?					

Table 9-1b. ISO 9001 Audit Questionnaire (cont'd)

A=acceptable   IN=insufficient   UN=unacceptable   NA=not applicable

Section IV Management of Support and Improvement	A	IN	UN	NA	Observations and objective evidence
105. Do you have a form specifically designed for reporting nonconforming products, and is it used?					
106. Do you have a form specifically designed for reporting nonconforming products, and is it used?					
107. Have you defined the responsibility for review, and the authority for disposition, of nonconforming products?					
108. Are repaired and reworked products reinspected in accordance with procedures or quality plans?					
109. Do you keep records of nonconforming products' disposition?					
4.14 Corrective and preventive action					
110. Do you study the root causes of product, process, and quality system nonconformities, and of customer complaints?					
111. Do you take the corrective actions needed to eliminate these root causes?					
112. Do you follow up on corrective actions to ensure their effective results?					
113. Do you analyze all quality-related information to discover and eliminate potential causes of nonconformities?					
114. Do you determine the steps needed to assess the risk of potential problems?					
115. Do you initiate preventive actions to resolve potential high-risk problems?					
116. Do you follow up on the effectiveness of preventive actions during management reviews?					
117. Do you modify the affected quality documentation as a result of actions taken?					

A=acceptable	IN=insufficient	UN=unacceptable	NA=not applicable

Section IV Management of Support and Improvement	A	IN	UN	NA	Observations and objective evidence
4.20 Statistical techniques					
118. Do you keep records of corrective and preventive actions taken?					
119. Are the needs for statistical techniques identified?					
120. Do you use tools and statistical techniques for receiving inspection? Do you have a procedure?					
121. Do you use tools and statistical techniques for in-process inspection? Do you have a procedure?					
122. Do you use tools and statistical techniques for final inspection? Do you have a procedure?					
123. Do you use tools and statistical techniques to improve processes? Do you have an appropriate guide?					
124. Do you use advanced statistical techniques to improve the product design process?					
125. Do you use statistical tools for the analysis of customer complaints?					
126. Do you use statistical tools for the analysis of internal nonconformities?					

Table 9-2a. Correlation between ISO 9004-2 Elements and the Sections of the Assessment Questionnaire for Service Organizations

ISO 9004-2 Elements* \ The Questionnaire Sections	I. Leadership	II. People Management	III. Quality System Management	IV. Management of the Customer Interface	V. Process Management	VI. Management of Improvement
4. Characteristics of services					✓	
4.1 Service and service delivery characteristics					✓	
4.2 Control of service and service delivery characteristics					✓	
5. Quality system principles	✓					
5.1 Key aspects of a quality system	✓					
5.2 Management responsibility	✓					
5.3 Personnel and material resources		✓				
5.4 Quality system structure	✓	✓	✓	✓	✓	✓
5.5 Interface with customers		✓		✓		
6. Quality system operational elements					✓	
6.1 Marketing process					✓	
6.2 Design process					✓	
6.3 Service delivery process					✓	✓
6.4 Service performance analysis and improvement						✓

* The element numbering is the same as in ISO 9004-2: 1991.

Table 9-2b. Assessment Questionnaire for Service Organizations

A=acceptable   IN=insufficient   UN=unacceptable   NA=not applicable

Section I Leadership	A	IN	UN	NA	Observations and objective evidence
1. Has executive management defined its role and responsibilities concerning the interface between customers, resources, and the quality system?					
2. Has your company adequately established a policy for service quality and customer satisfaction?					
3. Does the quality policy relate to the following elements: a. the grade of the service to be provided?					
b. the service organization's image?					
c. targets for service quality?					
d. the approach to attaining the targets?					
e. the company personnel's role?					
4. Is the quality policy understood, implemented, and maintained at all levels of the organization?					
5. Is the quality policy supported by precise quality goals?					
6. Are the goals sufficiently oriented toward: a. satisfaction of customers?					
b. continuous improvement of services?					
c. respect for society?					
d. protection of the environment?					
e. the efficiency of service delivery?					
7. Have you clearly defined the needs of the customer with the appropriate quality measures?					
8. Do you initiate preventive actions to avoid customer dissatisfaction?					

Table 9-2b. Assessment Questionnaire for Service Organizations (cont'd)

A=acceptable   IN=insufficient   UN=unacceptable   NA=not applicable

Section I Leadership	A	IN	UN	NA	Observations and objective evidence
9. Do you optimize costs of quality for the required service performance?					
10. Do you perform a continuous review of service requirements to identify opportunities for service quality improvement?					
11. Does your organization prevent adverse effects to society or to the environment?					
12. Do you have a management representative who ensures the implementation and continuous maintenance of the quality system?					
13. Do you conduct periodic management reviews to determine the performance of the quality system and opportunities for improvement?					
Section II People Management					
14. Do you have sufficient resources to implement the quality system?					
15. Do you select personnel on the basis of capability to satisfy definite job specifications?					
16. Do you provide a work environment that fosters excellence and the stability of work relationships?					
17. Does the organization provide each member with the opportunity for creative work and greater involvement?					
18. Are the tasks to be performed and goals to be achieved clearly understood by the employees?					
19. Do people feel involved in the quality of the service delivery?					
20. Do you have an employee recognition program to encourage contributions to service quality?					

A=acceptable	IN=insufficient	UN=unacceptable	NA=not applicable

Section II People Management	A	IN	UN	NA	Observations and objective evidence
21. Do you periodically assess the key factors that motivate people to provide service quality?					
22. Do you have adequate career planning for the development of personnel?					
23. Do you have training programs to update the skills of the personnel?					
24. Do you educate all employees on the company's quality policy, service goals, and customer satisfaction concept?					
25. Do you train executive in the principles and practices of quality management?					
26. Do you have a sensitization program on quality for new employees?					
27. Do you have a refresher program for the longer-serving personnel?					
28. Do you have training courses on:					
a. process control?					
b. problem identification and resolution?					
c. corrective and preventive actions?					
d. teamwork?					
e. communication methods?					
29. Do you have procedures to specify and verify the effectiveness of the training?					
30. Do you assess employee performance to determine development needs and evolution potential?					
31. Do employees who work directly with the customer have the necessary communication skills?					
32. Do you have an adequate and reliable information system?					
33. Are the necessary material resources available, adequate, effective, and maintained?					

Table 9-2b. Assessment Questionnaire for Service Organizations (cont'd)

| A=acceptable | IN=insufficient | UN=unacceptable | NA=not applicable |

Section III Management of the Quality System	A	IN	UN	NA	Observations and objective evidence
34. Have you established a quality manual containing: 　　a. the quality policy and service goals?					
b. the responsibilities?					
c. the structure of the service organization?					
d. the quality practices of the organization?					
e. the quality system requirements?					
35. Do you have a quality plan describing the quality practices, the resources, and the sequence of activities relevant to each service?					
36. Do you have procedures that describe the purpose, the scope, the methods, and the characteristics of activities in the service organization?					
37. Do you have quality records for: 　　a. the degree of achievement of the quality goals?					
b. the level of customer satisfaction?					
c. the analysis of quality trends?					
d. results of service quality?					
e. management reviews?					
f. internal audits and self-assessments?					
g. customers' assessments?					
h. corrective actions?					
i. the skills and training of the personnel?					
j. supplier performance?					
k. competitive comparisons?					
38. Do you have an established procedure for document and data control? Is it applied?					
39. Do you have an established procedure for internal quality audits? Is it applied?					

A=acceptable	IN=insufficient			UN=unacceptable	NA=not applicable

Section III Management of the Quality System	**A**	**IN**	**UN**	**NA**	**Observations and objective evidence**
40. Do you perform internal quality audits according to a preestablished schedule? Is it respected?					
41. During internal quality audits, do you follow up on the effectiveness of the corrective actions taken?					
Section IV Management of the Customer Interface					
42. Are the service characteristics clearly defined and subject to customer evaluation?					
43. Have you established an effective interaction between customers and your people, and is it assured?					
44. Do employees who have direct customer contact have the organizational freedom and responsibility to resolve problems and take appropriate action?					
45. Is the image of your company based on the reality of actions taken to satisfy customer needs?					
46. Do the employees, at all levels of the service organization, use this image in relationships with customers?					
47. Do you review the communication methods used to improve the interface with customers?					
48. Do you adequately provide to customers a detailed service description (scope, availability, timeliness, cost)?					
49. Do you effectively communicate to customers the relationship between the service, its delivery, and its cost?					
50. Do you effectively communicate to customers the manner in which eventual problems will be resolved?					

Table 9-2b. Assessment Questionnaire for Service Organizations (cont'd)

A=acceptable	IN=insufficient	UN=unacceptable	NA=not applicable

Section IV Management of the Customer Interface	A	IN	UN	NA	Observations and objective evidence
52. Do you use the customers' perception of service quality to improve your communication methods?					
53. Do you have effective communication means which are adapted and accessible to the customers?					
Section V **Management of Service Processes**					
The Marketing Process					
54. Have you established procedures for the planning and performing of market research and analysis activities?					
55. Are the obligations of your company towards its customers formally expressed?					
56. Once the decision to offer a service has been made, do you prepare a service brief?					
57. Have you established appropriate procedures for service management, and are they applied?					
58. Does the advertisement of a service reflect the service specification and take into account the customers' perception?					
The Design Process					
59. Do you have design specifications that are based on the service brief and that reflect the service goals, the quality policy, and the costs?					
60. Do you have a service specification that defines the characteristics of the service offered?					
61. Do you have a specification that defines the appropriate methods and means for the service delivery process?					
62. Do you have a procedure for the assessment of service characteristics?					

| A=acceptable | IN=insufficient | UN=unacceptable | NA=not applicable |

Section V Management of Service Processes	A	IN	UN	NA	Observations and objective evidence
63. Do you have a procedure for the control of service characteristics?					
64. Have you applied the principles of quality control in the development of the service and service delivery specifications?					
65. Are responsibilities adequately defined for all stages of the design process?					
66. Have you clearly specified the service characteristics that are subject to customer assessment?					
67. Have you clearly specified the service characteristics that are subject to self-assessment?					
68. Have you established standards of acceptability for all specified characteristics?					
69. Does the specification for service delivery adequately define: a. the characteristics that directly affect service performance?					
b. the standards of acceptability?					
c. the material resource requirements?					
d. the personnel resource requirements?					
e. the reliance on suppliers?					
70. Do the service delivery procedures adequately describe the following activities: a. communication of information?					
b. order taking?					
c. flowcharting of the service delivery process?					
d. billing and payment for the service?					
71. Have you adequately defined requirements concerning procurement for the service?					

Table 9-2b. Assessment Questionnaire for Service Organizations (cont'd)

A=acceptable	IN=insufficient	UN=unacceptable	NA=not applicable

Section V Management of Service Processes	A	IN	UN	NA	Observations and objective evidence
72. Do you have a procedure for the selection of suppliers and subcontractors, and is it respected?					
73. Do you control the supplier-provided equipment for use by customers?					
74. Is this equipment adapted to the needs of the customers and is it accompanied by clear user instructions?					
75. Have you established a procedure for effective control of the following activities: a. handling?					
b. storage?					
c. packaging?					
d. delivery?					
e. protection of customers' possessions?					
76. Have you established quality control specifications?					
77. Does the quality control involve: a. identification of the key activities in each service process?					
b. analysis of the key activities to select which characteristics to measure?					
c. definition of methods for the assessment of selected characteristics?					
d. development of means to control the characteristics within specified limits?					
78. Do you perform reviews at the end of each stage of the service design, carried out with respect to the service brief?					
79. Do the design reviews ensure that the service specifications satisfy customer requirements?					

A=acceptable	IN=insufficient	UN=unacceptable	NA=not applicable

Section V Management of Service Processes	A	IN	UN	NA	Observations and objective evidence
80. Do these design reviews ensure that the quality control specification is adequate?					
81. Do you validate new and modified services to ensure that they are fully developed and satisfy customer needs?					
82. Do you perform periodic revalidation to ensure that the services continue to meet customer needs?					
83. Do you control the service design changes?					
The Service Delivery Process					
84. Do you control the selected service delivery characteristics?					
85. Does the provision of services to customers adhere to the service delivery specifications, including process adjustments when a deviation occurs?					
86. Do the service quality assesments involve:					
a. measurement and verification of the key activities of the service delivery process?					
b. personnel self-inspection?					
c. internal assessment of the interface with customers?					
d. customer assessment of service quality?					
87. Have you established a permanent assessment and measure of customer satisfaction?					
88. Is there compatibility between the service brief, the service design, the service delivery, and the customer needs?					
89. Do you compare the customer assessment and your self-assessment of the service quality?					
90. Do you keep quality records of the work status at each phase of the service delivery process?					

Table 9-2b. Assessment Questionnaire for Service Organizations (cont'd)

A=acceptable	IN=insufficient	UN=unacceptable	NA=not applicable

Section VI Management of Improvement	A	IN	UN	NA	Observations and objective evidence
91. Does each person within the service organization have the duty and responsibility to discover and report nonconforming services?					
92. Are detected nonconformities recorded, analyzed, and corrected?					
93. Do you take corrective actions to eliminate the root cause of problems?					
94. Do you follow up on the effectiveness of corrective actions after their implementation?					
95. Do you have established procedures for controlling and maintaining the measurement system of service quality?					
96. Do you test the reliability and validity of the measuring and test equipment used in providing or assessing services?					
97. Do you use an appropriate reference (e.g., ISO 10012-1) as a guide for control of the measuring and test equipment?					
98. Do you test the reliability and validity of customer satisfaction surveys and questionnaires?					
99. Do you continually assess the operation of service processes to identify and actively pursue opportunities for service quality improvement?					
100. Do you have an information system allowing collection and distribution of data?					
101. Do the data available from measures of the service operation originate from the following means: a. the management review?					
b. the customers' assessment?					
c. the internal quality audits?					

A=acceptable	IN=insufficient	UN=unacceptable	NA=not applicable

Section VI Management of Improvement	A	IN	UN	NA	Observations and objective evidence
102. Do you systematically analyze the service achievement data to improve service quality and effectiveness?					
103. Do you use the selected data to establish a plan for service quality improvement?					
104. Do you use statistical methods to facilitate and optimize the data collection and analysis processes?					
105. Do you use statistical methods to identify customer needs?					
106. Do you use statistical methods for the control of service processes?					
107. Do you use statistical methods for the forecasting and measurement of quality?					
108. Do you have a program for continuous improvement (1) of the service quality and (2) of the effectiveness and efficiency of the service operation?					
109. Does your continuous improvement program involve the discovery of characteristics which if improved would most benefit the customer and the service organization?					
110. Does your continuous improvement program cover changing market needs?					
111. Does your continuous improvement program enable the discovery of deviations from the specified service quality?					
112. Does your continuous improvement program involve the discovery of cost reduction opportunities while improving service quality?					
113. Are the service improvement activities integrated with the short-term and longer-term improvement needs?					

Table 9-2b. Assessment Questionnaire for Service Organizations (cont'd)

A=acceptable   IN=insufficient   UN=unacceptable   NA=not applicable

Section VI Management of Improvement	A	IN	UN	NA	Observations and objective evidence
114. Do you identify relevant data for collection?					
115. Do you analyze potential problems that would have the greatest adverse impact on service quality?					
116. Do you initiate preventive actions to eliminate potential causes of high-risk problems?					
117. Do you give feedback of the analysis results to operational management with recommendations for immediate service improvement?					
118. Do you report information to executive management for periodic review of the service quality improvement process?					
119. Does executive management encourage people at all levels to contribute to the quality improvement program?					
120. Do you have a recognition process that encourages employee effort and participation in the quality improvement program?					
121. Do you have a reward system linked to the recognition process and to the results of the quality improvement program?					

10

Efficiency and Customization

Quality experts estimate that nonquality entails costs that can reach up to 20 percent of a manufacturing firm's sales. They can run as high as 35 percent for service companies such as banks and insurance firms.[1] It has been estimated that as many as half of the employees that work in the banking and insurance industry spend their time exclusively in correcting the mistakes of the other half.

The implementation of an ISO 9000 quality system decreases the cost of nonquality in companies. To be aware of a company's present situation and competitiveness, the cost of what is already in place must be measured. In fact, the solution is to assess the costs and effectiveness of the quality system in financial terms.

Costs of Quality

Internal quality audits can be accompanied by an assessment of the costs of quality. Companies can draw up a procedure that appraises quality-related costs presented in ISO 9004-1. This standard describes three methods to analyze the elements of financial data. The first, created by American guru Armand Feigenbaum, is the *quality costing method*. The second is the *process costing method*, which uses Philip Crosby's concepts of costs of conformity and costs of nonconformity. The third method is the *quality loss method*, which is founded on the loss function model of Japanese expert Genichi Taguchi.

Many companies in Europe and North America use the PAF (prevention, appraisal, failure) quality costing method.[2] According to this method each business unit, activity, department, or shop allocates its costs of quality to prevention and appraisal costs (investments), or internal and external failure costs (losses).

Prevention costs refer to management reviews, system audits, contract reviews, design reviews, personnel training, salaries of quality staff (management, quality engineering, quality auditing), prevention methods used in design and manufacturing, procedures, and overtime of the people involved in the prevention methods.

Appraisal costs include salaries of the persons who directly perform receiving, in-process and final inspection, design verification and validation, testing and calibration. Also included are the costs of the instruments and other means of appraisal, the procedures, the records, and the follow-up.

Internal failure costs concern nonconformities detected prior to delivery, such as from administration, information systems, marketing, production, procurement, defects studies, reperforming a service, reinspection and retest of repaired and reworked products, scrap, and breakdowns.

External failure costs encompass everything related to nonconformities that occur after delivery to customers. These costs include loss of actual and potential customers, product recalls, warranties and returns, installation and billing errors, repairs, and the time of personnel involved in these activities.

To measure the efficiency of their quality systems, companies use ratios such as:

- prevention costs / appraisal costs
- prevention costs / failure costs
- appraisal costs / failure costs
- internal failure costs / operating costs
- failure costs / sales

An assessment of the costs of quality will give management information regarding the efficiency of the quality system and of the prevention and appraisal methods used. Quality costs are hot indicators for quality improvement. Reports of quality costs are an excellent means for sensitizing top management to quality.

The three methods proposed by ISO 9004-1 for dealing with quality systems financial data have one drawback: they lack depth for practical application. They are centered around cost allocation and leave companies with the task of finding concrete tools for reducing the costs of nonquality.

Activity-Based Costing

In practice different approaches exist for the assessment of the costs of quality. A successful approach was carried out in the plants of Rhône Poulenc in France. Within a six-year span, the group doubled its business revenues thanks to a spectacular development of its market in the United States. Under the presidency of Jean-René Fourtou, who is also president of the French Movement for Quality, the company certified several of its European plants to ISO 9001. Today it is pursuing its efforts with a total quality policy.

From the outset Rhône Poulenc formed cost-quality teams that diagnosed the quality of the product. After analyzing the costing method, managers determined that product quality alone was not a sufficient measure of the total cost of quality. So the teams took into consideration the quality of the processes. This was done by valuing production stoppages and the resulting simultaneous effects in the process network, with the use of preestablished instrument panels. The quality director asserts that costs of quality become a tool for the management of process quality while taking into account reliability and availability, effectiveness, maintenance, and protection of the environment.[3]

Today companies have passed from the theoretical model to practical implementation. To ensure success in a quality costs analysis, it must be linked to the company's accounting system. The activity-based costing (ABC) and activity-based management (ABM) approaches account for hidden quality costs that were not considered in traditional accounting and management practices. Contrary to the traditional approach, where the company is viewed as a set of departmental units, ABC and ABM perceive the company as a set of processes and activities, for which cost evaluations can be made. These methods also make justification of an investment much easier. For example, ABC helped Caterpillar executives hang numbers on such intangibles as the value of better quality and faster time-to-market cycles; these numbers persuaded the board to approve a $2 billion plant-modernization drive that began in 1987.[4]

The ABC and ABM methods can be used to evaluate profitability of almost all the company's activities. More and more companies use computerized systems such as Manufacturing Resources Planning (MRP II) to plan and integrate their processes and resources. The broadening of MRP systems onto accounting activities allows the discovery of ABC method advantages.

Du Pont Canada is a good example of a company that has implemented a quality system in parallel with the adoption of new accounting methods. To become more competitive, the Fibers Division in Kingston, Ontario, adopted the ISO 9002[5] standard and integrated activity-based costing. In the past, each business division manager for this Du Pont plant was responsible for reducing costs in his or her area only. As a result, managers searched for the most advantageous cost allocation method, rather than focusing on cost reduction. The incentive was to reduce the business unit's costs, rather than the overall cost structure. When activity-based costing was introduced, production facilities and resources allocation methods became clearer. A software application now supplies up-to-the-minute online information and managers at the various sites can generate reports themselves at any given time. By implementing activity-based costing, Du Pont has redirected its focus of cost management from allocation to actually reducing the costs. The process has become more of a management process as opposed to a dollars process, and users can be more proactive in cost management. The result: Du Pont has increased profitability by controlling costs in the development of its products.[6]

Dynamize and Customize

An inconvenience of the ABC and ABM methods stems from the internal focus emphasized by accountants and the limited relation to process management and continuous improvement programs. The lack of integration of information, data, and requirements—formulated by customers, society in general, and the environment in particular—in cost analysis and process management constitutes an insufficiency for good implementation of these methods. The methods of financial analysis presented in the first subsection of this chapter cover certain aspects of the company's external environment (such as costs of conformity to customer requirements). But, they are static and can only serve as benchmarks.

While analyzing the advantages and disadvantages of financial data analysis methods and the ABC and ABM methods, I came up with the idea of combining their advantages to rebalance their drawbacks (see Figure 10-1). The solution I have developed is to *dynamize* the quality costs on one hand, and to *customize* the processes on the other hand. This customization integrates the requirements of customers, environment, and society in processes. Such dynamics and customization will allow assessment of the conformity and efficiency of each process and will help drive the discovery of activities for improvement or redesign. This reinvented model will enable the process manager to use concrete and complete data, supplied and analyzed by cost accounting.

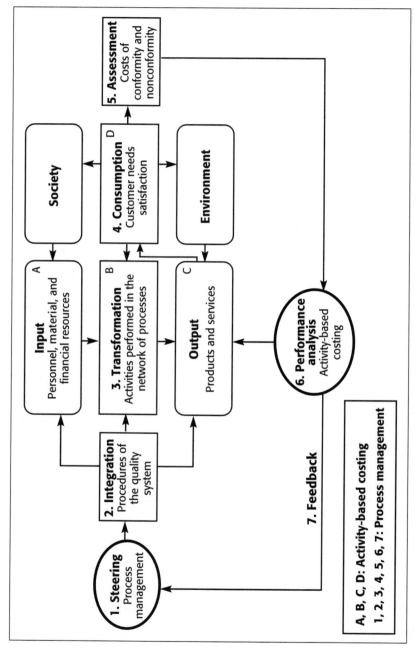

Figure 10-1. Customized Cost Management

Notes

1. Philip Crosby, *Quality Without Tears*, New York: Plume/New American Library, 1984, p. 5.

2. ISO, *ISO 9000 Compendium*, 5th edition, 1994, p. 187.

3. Patrick Bertin, "Le coût d'obtention de la qualité," *Informations Chimie*, no. 325, January-February 1991, p. 167-170.

4. Kevin Kelly, "A Bean-Counter's Best Friend," *Business Week/Quality*, January 1992, p. 42-43.

5. QMI, *The Corporate Quality Guide*, Mississauga, Ontario: QMI, December 1992.

6. Bryan Plug, "Bringing Quality to Accounting," *CMA Magazine*, July-August 1992, p. 17-19.

11

Improvements in ISO 9000: 1994

The new economic era has moved businesses to rethink management concepts, market strategies, and business processes. Revision of the five standards of the ISO 9000 series is done on average every five years and it follows, of course, the evolution of global market requirements and management thinking, and the boom of information technology. The new edition of the ISO 9000 series saw the light in July 1994. The improvements incorporated suggestions from companies that had used and implemented these standards during the six years before, as well as from international experts who track the quality concept evolution (see "Quality Concepts Road Map" in Chapter 3).

Improvements to the Quality Assurance Requirements

The numbering used in the ISO 9001, ISO 9002 and ISO 9003: 1994 standards remains identical to that in the previous edition. Like the previous version, ISO 9001: 1994 contains 20 requirements, many of which have been reinforced and improved (see Table 11-1). The ISO 9002: 1994 model contains 19 requirements and the processes are broadened to include servicing. The ISO 9003: 1994 model includes four new requirements: contract review, control of customer-supplied product, corrective action, and internal audits.

Improvements to the Quality Management Guidelines

The new ISO 9004-1 standard, which replaces ISO 9004: 1987, still gives guidelines for quality system elements to guide companies. The new standard clarifies the life cycle of the product, adds the element of quality improvement, and makes reference to the new norms. Table 11-2 presents a synthesis of the improvements to the ISO 9004-1 guidelines.

Trends

The next edition of the ISO 9000 standards will probably be published in 1999. This second revision, which is called Phase II, has already been started by the ISO/TC 176, and is considered major. According to committee reports, work on the future edition has progressed well. The evolution of total quality management has been examined in detail, and a work group (SC2/WG15 led by ANSI) is in charge of the issue. The future ISO 9004-8 norm will provide guidelines on quality in business practices in *Guidelines on Quality Principles and their Application to Management Practices*.[1]

The long-term objectives of the International Organization for Standardization concerning the ISO 9000 series are:

- a single standard for quality management principles (an updated ISO 9004-1)
- a single standard for quality management practices (using ISO 9004-1 as a starting point)
- a single standard on requirements for quality assurance assessment (an updated ISO 9001)[2]

These objectives demonstrate ISO's will to integrate the concepts and simplify the architecture throughout these new standards to facilitate their application in the business world.

Table 11-1. ISO 9001: 1994 Improvements

The 20 Requirements of ISO 9001	Improvements of ISO 9001: 1994
4.1 Management responsibility	Executive management responsibility is required for implementation of the quality system.
4.1.1 Quality policy	The quality policy must reflect the organizational goals and the customers' needs and expectations. The quality objectives and commitment of executive management are included in the quality policy.
4.1.2 Organization	Authority and freedom are required for disposition of nonconformities of products, of processes, and of the quality system. The organization now involves people who manage and perform work, not only verification personnel.
4.1.3 Management review	Intervals between management reviews must be defined.
4.2 Quality system 4.2.1 General	The quality manual must now reflect the corporate quality policy, the organization, and include the structure of the documentation of the quality system.
4.2.2 Quality system procedures	Quality procedures are required according to the elements of the standard and the stated quality policy.
4.2.3 Quality planning	This new section covers quality planning of quality systems and products. Quality plans are now included for products, projects, or contracts.
4.3 Contract review	The review of contracts and orders before acceptance is required, as is the review of tenders before submission. Amendments to contracts must be correctly transferred to the functions concerned within the organization.
4.4 Design control*	Design reviews, verifications, and validations are now distinct activities and are performed at the different stages of design. Multiple validations may be performed if there are different intended uses.

* This requirement is not part of the ISO 9002 and ISO 9003 standards.
  Source: *ISO 9001*, 1994.

The 20 Requirements of ISO 9001	Improvements of ISO 9001: 1994
4.5 Document and data control	This requirement applies to hard copy and electronic media. Obsolete documents must be removed or otherwise protected against unintentional use. Retention of properly identified obsolete documents, to demonstrate the effective operation of the quality system, is now acceptable.
4.6 Purchasing**	The company now selects subcontractors according to the quality assurance requirements (concerning the product and the quality system). Verification and release arrangements of the purchased product are clarified.
4.7 Control of customer-supplied product	The term "purchaser" has been replaced by the term "customer." Responsibilities concerning the customer-supplied product are clarified.
4.8 Product identification and traceability	
4.9 Process control**	This clause applies to all processes, from production and installation to servicing. Control of process parameters and of product characteristics is required. Workmanship criteria must be defined clearly. Equipment maintenance is required to ensure continuing process capability.
4.10 Inspection and testing	A new section now requires documented procedures and/or quality plans concerning product verification activities. The criteria concerning the nature and breadth of inspection and testing must be defined and recorded. Records must prove that the inspected or tested product has passed or failed according to defined acceptance criteria.
4.11 Control of inspection, measuring, and test equipment	A new section describes the elements of a procedure dealing with the control of measuring equipment. The control, maintenance, and validation of test software and test hardware are included. Measuring equipment for servicing is included.

** This requirement is not part of the ISO 9003 standard.

Table 11-1. ISO 9001: 1994 Improvements (cont'd)

The 20 Requirements of ISO 9001	Improvements of ISO 9001: 1994
4.12 Inspection and test status	A written procedure is now required for identification of the inspection and test status (indicating conformance or nonconformance of the product) with suitable means.
4.13 Control of nonconforming product	The repaired and/or reworked product must be reinspected.
4.14 Corrective and preventive action	Documented procedures for corrective and preventive actions must be established. These actions are separated into two sections.
4.14.1 Corrective action	The effective handling of customer complaints and nonconformity reports is now required. Corrective actions must investigate, discover, and eliminate the root causes of nonconformities of the product, the processes, and the system.
4.14.2 Preventive action**	Preventive actions aim to eliminate the causes of potential nonconformities. The steps for taking preventive actions must be predetermined. Follow-up must be performed during management reviews.
4.15 Handling, storage, packaging, preservation, and delivery	Preservation is separated from packaging, and all activities must be documented by procedures.
4.16 Control of quality records	A documented procedure is required.
4.17 Internal quality audits	Documented procedures are required for the planning, performing, and reporting of internal audits and the *follow-up* of the effectiveness of the resulting actions. The clause makes a reference to the ISO 10011 guidelines for conducting quality system audits.
4.18 Training	
4.19 Servicing**	Procedures must now be documented for performing, verifying, and reporting that the servicing meets the specified requirements.
4.20 Statistical techniques	The need for statistical techniques must be identified. Implementation of statistical techniques must be performed according to documented procedures.

** This requirement is not part of the ISO 9003 standard.

Table 11-2. ISO 9004-1: 1994 Improvements

The purpose and scope of the new ISO 9004-1 standard are the same as before, to provide quality management guidance. ISO 9004-1:1994 also presents new concepts on quality management and process-based management. All activities can be considered as processes with inputs and outputs. Planning and prevention are emphasized. The life cycle of a product is clarified and importance is put on market study, market follow-up, and market feedback. Environmental considerations and quality improvement concepts are added.

Contents	Improvements
0. Introduction	It is clearly indicated that the ISO 9004-1 standard is not intended for contractual or certification purposes, nor for ISO 9001, ISO 9002, or ISO 9003 implementation guidance. Its purpose is to describe what elements quality systems should encompass, not to enforce their uniformity.
1. Scope	The term "quality management system" has been replaced by the term "quality system."
2. Normative references	The new ISO 9004-2, ISO 9004-3, and ISO 9004-4 standards are included as references.
3. Definitions	The relationships of organizations in the supply chain of processes are defined.
4. Management responsibility	
5. Quality system elements	The term "phases in the quality loop" has been replaced by the term "phases in the life cycle." After sales and market feedback are added in the life cycle of the product. Recycling is the final phase of the life cycle. Quality improvement is included as a new element of the quality system (section 5.6) and a reference is made to the new ISO 9004-4 standard. Configuration management (section 5.2.6) is included in the structure of the quality system.
6. Financial considerations of quality systems	Three approaches are introduced for financial reporting of quality system activities: quality-cost approach, process-cost approach, and quality-loss approach (see Chapter 10).
7. Quality in marketing	

Source: *ISO 9004-1*, 1994.

Table 11-2. ISO 9004-1: 1994 Improvements (cont'd)

Contents	Improvements
8. Quality in specification and design	
9. Quality in purchasing	
10. Quality in processes	Packaging (section 10.1.5) and handling (section 10.4) are included.
11. Control of processes	A new section deals with process control management and replaces special processes.
12. Product verification	
13. Control of inspection, measuring, and test equipment	
14. Control of nonconforming product	
15. Corrective action	
16. Post-production activities	The post-production activities (clause 16) are now: storage, delivery, installation, servicing, after sales, and market feedback.
17. Quality records	
18. Personnel	
19. Product safety	
20. Use of statistical methods	

Notes

1. ISO/TC 176.

2. Kerry Somerset, "Phase 2 Revisions and Needs of Small Businesses," *ISO 9000 News*, vol. 3, no. 4, July-August 1994.

12

ISO 9000 and the Harmonization
of Other Standardization

The Big Three's Big Step

ISO 9000: 1994 has intensified its requirements regarding preventive action and quality planning for the operation of a quality system. One of the most tangible results was the birth of the Big Three's QS-9000 quality system and its downstream impact on the worldwide automotive business.

QS-9000 is the new quality system standard for the North American automotive industry. Developed by Chrysler, Ford, and General Motors, the QS-9000 quality system model harmonizes ISO 9000 with Chrysler's Supplier Quality Assurance Manual, Ford's Q101 quality system standard, and GM's Targets for Excellence standard for supplier performance evaluation.

QS-9000 represents a leap in the standardization history of the automotive industry. The Big Three's big step aims to strengthen competitiveness in the world marketplace, to benchmark against ISO

9000, and to provide commonality and compatibility for thousands of external and internal auto suppliers. In addition to being used by General Motors, Ford and Chrysler, QS-9000 has also been adopted by several truck manufacturers, including Freightliner, Mack Trucks, Navistar, Paccar, the Transportation Manufacturing Corporation, and Volvo/GM.[1]

The QS-9000 quality manual includes ISO 9001 requirements as well as sector-specific requirements and customer-specific requirements (see Tables 12-1 and 12-2). The sector-specific requirements apply specifically to the automotive industry whereas the customer-specific requirements represent the individual requests that Chrysler, Ford, and General Motors have formulated for their suppliers.

By standardizing their business practices to satisfy the Big Three's quality system requirements, auto suppliers no longer need to satisfy individual customer requests nor receive a number of redundant assessments. In my experience working for a supplier of ABS brake systems to ten of the largest European, North American, and Japanese automakers, we had to comply to different requirements for each one. This arrangement was a heavy burden for the buyers as well as the supplier. The differences between the standards, the specific requirements, and the assessment process of each automaker did not necessarily contribute to quality improvement and raised the need for a common quality system standard and assessment process for the automotive industry.

According to *Quality Progress*, in December 1994 representatives from Chrysler, Ford, General Motors, two accreditation bodies, and 36 third-party ISO 9000 registrars met in Detroit to determine the registration process to QS-9000 requirements. This process has two steps:

Step 1. The prospective registrar provides its accreditation body or bodies with a completed application, including information on how it will satisfy additional QS-9000 requirements as outlined in the QS-9000 manual. Accreditation bodies include the United States' RAB, the Netherlands' RvC, and the United Kingdom's NACCB.

Step 2. An accreditation body recognized by one of the Big Three automakers serves as an on-site witness of a registrar's QS-9000 assessment of a supplier. After a notice of approval has been received, the registrar is then QS-9000 qualified and can certify suppliers to QS-9000 and ISO 9000.[2]

The list of QS-9000 qualified registrars and the QS-9000 manual are available from the ASQC, the RAB, and the Automotive Industry Action Group (AIAG).

Harmonization of ISO 9000 with the Defense Industry

Most companies from the defense industry in NATO member countries already have a quality system in compliance with the AQAP standards, whose most complete model is AQAP-1. In comparison with ISO 9001, in the military model responsibilities fall mostly on the Quality Assurance Representative (QAR), and identification and traceability of the product, internal audits, training, and servicing are not required. Tables 12-3 and 12-4 compare the 20 requirements of ISO 9001 with the ones from the AQAP-1 series and those from the MIL-Q-9858A series (the old standard of the U.S. Department of Defense, from which all quality assurance standards originate).

Table 12-1. QS-9000/ISO 9000 Cross-Element Comparison

QS-9001/ISO 9001 Requirements	QS-9002/ISO 9002 Requirements
4.1　Management responsibility	✔
4.1.1 Quality policy	✔
4.1.2 Organization	✔
4.1.3 Management review	✔
4.2　Quality system	✔
4.3　Contract review	✔
4.4　Design control	
4.5　Document and data control	✔
4.6　Purchasing	✔
4.7　Control of customer-supplied product	✔
4.8　Product identification and traceability	✔
4.9　Process control	✔
4.10 Inspection and testing	✔
4.11 Control of inspection, measuring, and test equipment	✔
4.12 Inspection and test status	✔
4.13 Control of nonconforming product	✔
4.14 Corrective and preventive action	✔
4.15 Handling, storage, packaging, preservation, and delivery	✔
4.16 Control of quality records	✔
4.17 Internal quality audits	✔
4.18 Training	✔
4.19 Servicing	✔
4.20 Statistical techniques	✔

Note: The ISO 9001 and ISO 9002 models are fully incorporated in the QS-9001/2 models. The ISO 9003 model is not recognized.

Table 12-2. Additional Requirements of the QS-9000 Standards

QS-9000 Sector-Specific Requirements
Production Part Approval Process (PPAP)
1.1 General
1.2 Engineering change validation
Continuous Improvement
2.1 General
2.2 Quality and productivity improvements
2.3 Techniques for continuous improvement
Manufacturing Capabilities
3.1 Facilities, equipment, and process planning and effectiveness
3.2 Mistake-proofing
3.3 Tool design and fabrication
3.4 Tooling management
QS-9000 Customer-Specific Requirements
Chrysler's requirements
Ford's requirements
General Motors' requirements

Table 12-3. QS-9001/AQAP-1 Cross-Element Comparison

The 20 Requirements of ISO 9001: 1994	Corresponding Sections of AQAP-1 (Edition 3-1984)
4.1 Management responsibility (executive)	201, 202, and 203-QAR
4.2 Quality system	205
4.3 Contract review	204
4.4 Design control	207
4.5 Document and data control	208
4.6 Purchasing	210
4.7 Control of customer-supplied product	212
4.8 Product identification and traceability	
4.9 Process control	211
4.10 Inspection and testing	213
4.11 Control of inspection, measuring, and test equipment	209
4.12 Inspection and test status	216
4.13 Control of nonconforming product	215
4.14 Corrective and preventive action	206
4.15 Handling, storage, packaging, preservation, and delivery	217
4.16 Control of quality records	205
4.17 Internal quality audits	
4.18 Training	
4.19 Servicing	
4.20 Statistical techniques	214 Sampling plans

* The bold type indicates a major difference between the two standards.

Table 12-4. QS-9001/MIL-Q9858A Cross-Element Comparison

The 20 Requirements of ISO 9001: 1994	Corresponding Sections of MIL-Q-9858A
4.1 Management responsibility (executive)*	3.1
4.2 Quality system	1.3 and 3.1
4.3 Contract review	3.2
4.4 Design control	4.1
4.5 Document and data control	4.1
4.6 Purchasing	5.1 and 5.2
4.7 Control of customer-supplied product	7.2
4.8 Product identification and traceability	4.8 and 6.7
4.9 Process control	3.3 and 6.2
4.10 Inspection and testing	6.1, 6.3, and 7.1
4.11 Control of inspection, measuring, and test equipment	4.2, 4.3, 4.4, and 4.5
4.12 Inspection and test status	6.7
4.13 Control of nonconforming product	6.5
4.14 Corrective and **preventive** action	3.5
4.15 Handling, storage, packaging, preservation, and delivery	6.4
4.16 Control of quality records	3.4
4.17 Internal quality audits	
4.18 Training	
4.19 Servicing	
4.20 Statistical techniques	6.6
Costs of Quality (ISO 9004-1)	3.6

* The bold type indicates a major difference between the two standards.

Notes

1. Jon Brecka, "QS-9000 Activities Heating Up," *Quality Progress*, April 1995, p. 20.

2. "Criteria Set for Those Wishing to Serve as Third-Party Registrars for QS-9000," *Quality Progress*, March 1995, p. 21.

13
The Quality Oscars

Quality Awards

The worldwide quality initiative of ISO is conducted in parallel with national quality initiatives around the world. These are the criteria used in organized competitions for awards and recognition—the Oscars of the quality world. Every year since 1987 the president of the United States presents the Malcolm Baldrige National Quality Award. In Europe, the annual European Quality Award was bestowed for the first time in 1992 by the king of Spain, Juan Carlos I. Japan has awarded the Deming Application Prize annually since 1951. In Canada, the Excellence Award for Quality is bestowed yearly. Each of these awards is based on a comprehensive set of criteria covering many facets of quality management. Many companies that never apply for these awards nevertheless use the criteria to shape their quality programs.

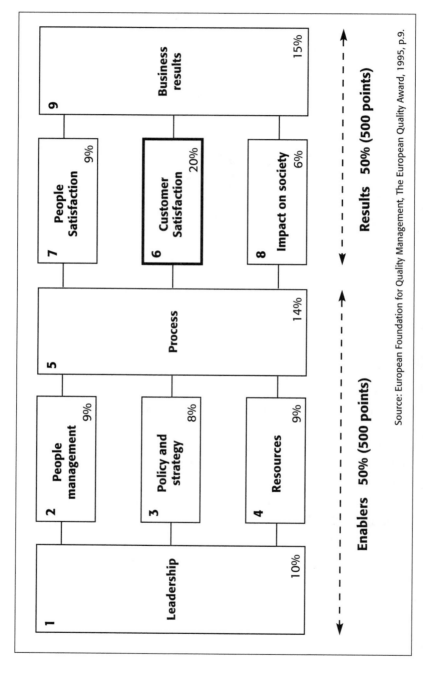

Source: European Foundation for Quality Management, The European Quality Award, 1995, p.9.

Figure 13-1. The European Model for Total Quality Management

It may be useful to highlight the particularities of the world's four best-known awards. The European model for total quality management emphasizes society, people and customer satisfaction, and business results (see Figure 13-1). The Canadian framework for effective organizations targets customer, employee, investor, and supplier satisfaction.[1] The Japanese Deming Prize, for its part, promotes quality assurance and continuous quality improvement through statistical quality control. Finally, the Malcolm Baldrige framework (see Figure 13-2)[2] emphasizes customer-driven quality and business results through strategic quality planning, competitive comparisons, and benchmarking. The approaches of each of these quality models and the ISO 9000 family are compared in Table 13-1.

Table 13-1. Quality Oscars Snapshot

Model	Approach	Outcomes
Deming Application Prize	Total quality control	Companywide and supplier quality improvement
Malcolm Baldrige National Quality Award	Quality of management	Customer satisfaction and competitiveness
European Quality Award	Total quality management	Customer/employee/community satisfaction and business results
Canadian Excellence Award for Quality	Total quality management	Customer/employee/supplier/ investor satisfaction
ISO 9000 family	Quality principles in management practices	Customer/employee/owner/ supplier and society confidence

Malcolm Baldrige and ISO 9004-1: A Comparative Study

In the United States the most popular quality initiatives are the ISO 9000 standards and the Malcolm Baldrige National Quality Award. The Baldrige quality management approach is more aggressive than ISO quality management for competitive comparison, benchmarking, and strategic planning. The ISO 9000 approach is more structured and detailed than the Baldrige Award for process management, quality system configuration, quality system assessment, use of statistical methods, and worldwide customer-supplier relationships.

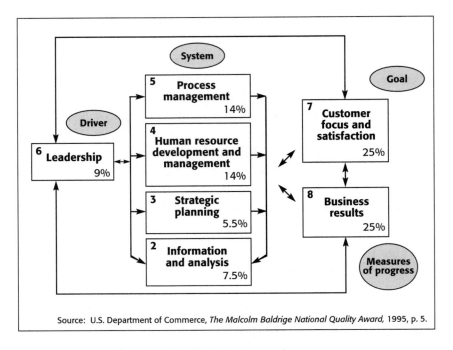

Source: U.S. Department of Commerce, *The Malcolm Baldrige National Quality Award*, 1995, p. 5.

Figure 13-2. Baldrige Award Criteria Framework

"Standards are critically important to the bottom line of every corporation in the United States," comments Motorola CEO Gary Tooker. "In this interconnected world, standards can play a pivotal role in enabling U.S. companies to effectively compete and win in the global marketplace."[3]

As shown in a study conducted by the Institute of Management Accountants (IMA) in the United States, 35 percent of interviewed CEOs consider ISO 9000 very important and only 17 percent grant the same importance to the Baldrige program. Interest in the international standards results from their worldwide success, compared with Baldrige, "which is more a beauty contest and not necessarily attractive to everyone."[4]

Perhaps in a more perfect world, muses a *Fortune* magazine article, the Baldrige criteria—which do demand quality products, satisfied customers, and continuous improvement—would become the international quality standard. However, even winning the Baldrige Award is no guarantee of commercial success; Wallace Company, a small pipe and valve distributor, won the prize in 1990 and filed for Chapter 11 the following year.[5]

The Baldrige award program received 586 applications from U.S. companies during the past few years. In 1995 only 43 companies applied, down from 106 companies in 1991. A recent report by The Conference Board says that a majority of large U.S. firms have used the criteria of the Baldrige award for self-improvement and the evidence suggests a long-term link between use of the Baldrige criteria and improved business performance.[6]

In any case, the purpose here is not to disparage either approach but to highlight differences and areas for potential improvement, based on my analysis of correlations between the Baldrige Award and the ISO 9004-1 standard as shown in Table 13-2.

Many studies compare the Baldrige criteria to the 20 ISO 9001 requirements and minimize the exhaustivity of the ISO 9000 family. In 1995 the ISO 9000 family contains 20 standards (not 20 requirements) and the generic standards are the ISO 9000-1 road map and the ISO 9004-1 quality management guidelines. For its part, the improved 1995 Baldrige criteria contain seven key areas of business performance, including 24 basic requirements.

Table 13-2 details the cross-section correspondence between the 24 requirements of the 1995 Baldrige Award criteria and the elements of the ISO 9004-1: 1994 guidelines for quality management. Only two requirements of Baldrige do not have parallel elements in the ISO 9004-1 model, and only two ISO elements do not correspond to any Baldrige criterion. The compatibility of the corresponding requirements varies from a limited to a higher degree and the global compatibility of the two models is greater than 75 percent.

Table 13-2. Baldrige/ISO 9004-1 Cross Element Comparison

The 24 Sections of the Malcolm Baldrige National Quality Award (1995)	Corresponding Sections of the ISO 9004-1 Quality Management Guidelines
1.1 Senior executive leadership	4. Management responsibility
1.2 Leadership system and organization	4. Management responsibility 5. Quality system elements
1.3 Public responsibility and corporate citizenship	4. Management responsibility
2.1 Management of information and data	5. Quality system elements 17. Quality records
2.2 Competitive comparisons and benchmarking	(See ISO 9004-4 guidelines for quality improvement)
2.3 Analysis and use of company-level data	5.4 Auditing the quality system 5.5 Review and evaluation of the quality system 5.6 Quality improvement 17. Quality records
3.1 Strategy development	4. Management responsibility
3.2 Strategy deployment	5. Quality system elements 5.1 Extent of application 5.2 Structure of the quality system 5.3 Documentation of the quality system
4.1 Human resource planning and evaluation	18. Personnel
4.2 High performance work systems	18.3 Motivation
4.3 Employee education, training, and development	18.1 Training 18.2 Qualification
4.4 Employee well-being and satisfaction	18.3 Motivation
5.1 Design and introduction of product and services	8. Quality in specification and design
5.2 Process management: product and service production	10. Quality in process 11. Control of process 12. Product verification 16. Post-production activities

The 24 Sections of the Malcolm Baldrige National Quality Award (1995)	Corresponding Sections of the ISO 9004-1 Quality Management Guidelines
5.3 Process management: support services	13. Control of inspection, measuring, and test equipment 14. Control of nonconforming product 15. Corrective action 5.4 Auditing the quality system
5.4 Management of supplier performance	9. Quality in purchasing
6.1 Product and service quality results	16.5 After sales 16.6 Market feedback
6.2 Company operational and financial results	6. Financial consideration of quality systems
6.3 Supplier performance results	17. Quality records 9. Quality in purchasing
7.1 Customer and market knowledge	7. Quality in marketing
7.2 Customer relationship management	7. Quality in marketing 16. Post-production activities
7.3 Customer satisfaction determination	7.3 Customer feedback information 16.4 Servicing 16.5 After sales
7.4 Customer satisfaction results	16.5 After sales 16.6 Market feedback
7.5 Customer satisfaction comparison	
	19. Product safety
	20. Use of statistical methods

The ISO 9004-4 Guidelines for Quality Improvement

The ISO 9004-4 guidelines provide principles for managing and implementing continuous quality improvement within an organization. They propose the fundamental concepts, the management approach, the methodology for quality improvement, and 11 supporting tools.

The guidelines clarify the scope of the quality improvement goals for companies: "They should be closely integrated with the overall business goals and provide focus for increasing customer satisfaction." Quality improvement must be planned and organized within a structured approach that uses data collection and analysis. This approach usually starts with the search for and identification of improvement opportunities, continues with the establishment of cause and effect relationships, and is completed with problem solutions and implementation of improvement actions. ISO 9004-4 recognizes that quality improvement is achieved through the continuous improvement of processes. It proposes the Shewhart cycle (PDCA: plan-do-check-act) for continuous improvement and emphasizes the check-act phases of this cycle[7] (see Figure 13-3). Quality improvement projects can be complex and require the intervention of senior management. They can also be relatively simple and be put in place by employee teams as part of their usual work.

The ISO 9004-4 quality improvement guidelines favor teamwork and recommend a recognition process that is in parallel with the reward system. They warn to avoid a reward system that favors destructive internal competition. Overall, the continuous improvement process leads to the implementation of new measures and indicators in order to assess the new performance level.

Internal quality system audits, management reviews, or regular self-assessments are powerful tools since they allow companies to build and maintain a continuous quality improvement process. According to Chairman Bernard Fournier of Rank Xerox, the first company to win the European Quality Award, also registered ISO 9000, "the self-evaluating process, like the self-appraisal requirement for the Award application, is a very valuable exercise because it integrates the quality closed loop of action-check-result. The Award's self-appraisal approach forces you to evaluate everything in the company and see exactly where you have weaknesses, and gives you an opportunity to address those faults."[8]

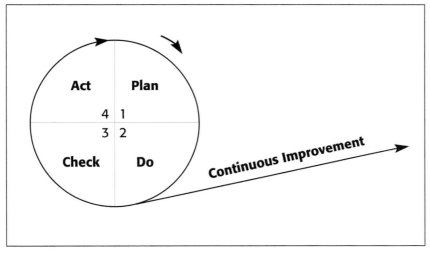

Figure 13-3. The Shewhart PDCA Cycle for Continuous Improvement

Notes

1. Industry Canada, *Entry Guide for the Canada Awards for Excellence*, 1995.

2. United States Department of Commerce, *Malcolm Baldrige National Quality Award*, 1995.

3. Gary Tooker, vice chairman and CEO of Motorola, Comments made during the celebration of World Standards Day in the United States, Washington, D.C., October 11, 1994.

4. Dirk Dusharme, "ISO 9000 Scores Higher than Baldrige Award," *Quality Digest*, February 1993, p. 7.

5. Ronald Henkoff, "The Hot New Seal of Quality," *Fortune*, June 28, 1993, p. 117-118.

6. U.S. Department of Commerce, "Delivering results: A progress report from the NIST," June 1995, p. 9.

7. ISO, *ISO 9000 Compendium*, 5th edition, 1994, p. 255.

8. "Interview: Bernard Fournier, Rank Xerox," *Quality Link* 4, no. 21, December 1992, p. 5.

14

Green Management

Integration of Management Systems

The environment is one of the levers of prosperity for modern society and the planet, and will be one of the priorities of the twenty-first century. Several companies, professional associations, governments, standardization committees, international bodies, voluntary movements, and universities, among others, are searching for effective ways to protect the environment. The actual environmental legislation may grow stronger; laws, requirements, and technical specifications will evolve in parallel with technological progress. But how does a company manage its environmental requirements while satisfying ecologists and owners, employees and customers, registrars and governments? And how does a company go beyond this satisfaction to protect the environment in a real, effective, and efficient manner?

Most companies still manage safety, quality, environmental, technological, and human resource problems separately. In the past, actions for the protection of the environment were rarely taken from a preventive standpoint. Rather, they were taken as emergency measures and in a reactive, corrective, and static manner, despite their high costs and ineffectiveness. Can we repair the hole in the ozone layer? Can we heal the victims of a nuclear catastrophy such as Chernobyl? The wish of international specialists in this field is "to integrate these policies, programs, and practices fully into each business as an essential element of management in all its functions."[1] This integral approach consolidates the company's environmental and safety systems with its quality system, in view of establishing a dynamic management system that is preventive, effective, and efficient.

The quality management concept proposed by the ISO 9000 standards facilitates the development of environmental management. In North America, the Monsanto plant in Montreal was one of the first chemical companies to obtain ISO 9001 certification including environmental requirements. In Europe, the British Standards Institution (BSI) recognized, in March 1992, the natural link between the BS 7750 standard for environmental management and the ISO 9000 series. Following a pilot project in which more than 200 companies participated, BSI adopted BS 7750 as the United Kingdom's national standard. However, according to Canadian experts, this standard is better applied to large companies; simplifications are required to apply it to small businesses.

ISO 14000 for Environment Protection

The analogy between the ISO 9000 and environmental management concepts lies in the *preventive approach of the quality system and in its continuous support and improvement* by internal audits, management reviews, and corrective and preventive actions. Development of the ISO 14000 series of international standards for environmental management systems, with this same approach, will allow companies to more effectively and economically protect the environment. According to Lawrence Eicher, Secretary General of

ISO, the elaboration of environmental standards is one of the organization's top priorities. "Industry is supporting the development of environmental standards for the purpose of trying to do its own self-regulation and to avoid regulation that would be done by governments in the environmental area."[2] The international standards will also decrease the multiplication of external eco-audits.

In 1993, ISO formed a new technical committee, ISO/TC 207, to draw up international standards for environmental management systems (EMS). Canada was given responsibility for presidence and secretariat of this committee. ISO/TC 207 is divided into six subcommittees (SC). The United Kingdom (SC 1) is coordinating the development of environmental management systems (ISO 14004 and ISO 14001); the Netherlands (SC 2) is in charge of the standards for environmental auditing (ISO 14010-12); Australia (SC 3), environmental labeling (ISO 14020-24); the United States (SC 4), environmental performance evaluation (ISO 14031); France (SC 5), life cycle assessment (ISO 14041); and Norway (SC 6), terms and definitions (ISO 14050).[3] Normally the draft standard of each subcommittee should become an international standard, approved by at least 75 percent of the technical committee members. These standards should become the ISO 14000 series and be published in mid-1996. Table 14-1 gives the cross-section correspondence between ISO 14001 and ISO 9001.

Simultaneously, the European Community has developed the CEMAS (European Community Environmental Management and Audit Standard) program for voluntary eco-audit. It will be introduced in 1995 (annual eco-report, periodic eco-assessments, independence of auditors).[4] The requirements of this program are similar to the principles of the ISO 9000 standards, notably for environmental policies and objectives, the manual, and the procedures. The eco-audit program requires a third-party verification. The launching of the CEMAS program reinforces the need for international standards. The ISO 14000 standards will avoid the eventual gap between the European and North American standards on one hand, and will counterbalance environmental regulation on the other. Coherence between ISO and

Table 14-1. Correspondence between ISO 9001 and ISO 14001

The ISO 9001 requirements	The ISO 14001 requirements*
4.1 Management responsibility 4.1.1 Quality policy	4.1 Environmental policy
	4.2 Planning 4.2.1 Environmental aspects 4.2.2 Legal and other requirements 4.2.3 Objectives and targets 4.2.4 Environmental management programs
4.1.2 Organization	4.3.1 Structure and responsibility
4.1.3 Management review	4.5 Management review
4.2 Quality system 4.2.1 General	4.0 General
	4.3.3 Communications
4.2.2 Quality system procedures	4.3.4 Environmental documentation 4.3.6 Operational Control
4.2.3 Quality planning	
4.3 Contract review	4.3.6 Operational control
4.4 Design control	4.3.6 Operational control
4.5 Document and data control	4.3.5 Document control
4.6 Purchasing	4.3.6 Operational control
4.7 Control of customer-supplied product	4.3.6 Operational control
4.8 Product identification and traceability	
4.9 Process control	4.3.6 Operational control
4.10 Inspection and testing	4.4.1 Monitoring and measurement
4.11 Control of inspection, measuring, and test equipment	4.4.1 Monitoring and measurement
4.12 Inspection and test status	
4.13 Control of nonconforming product	4.4.2 Nonconformance and corrective preventive action
4.14 Corrective and preventive action	4.4.2 Nonconformance and corrective preventive action
	4.3.7 Emergency preparedness and response
4.15 Handling, storage, packaging, preservation, and delivery	4.3.6 Operational control
4.16 Control of quality records	4.4.3 Records
4.17 Internal quality audits	4.4.4 Environmental management system audit
4.18 Training	4.3.2 Training, awareness, and competence
4.19 Servicing	4.3.6 Operational control
4.20 Statistical techniques	

Source: ISO/DIS 14001. Environmental Management Systems–specification for guidance for use.
* Note: As of September, 1995, the ISO/DIS is a draft international standard and certain requirements are subject to change

CEMAS can be assured by BSI, which coordinates both committees. Finally, ISO 14004: *Environmental Management Systems—General Guidelines on Principles, Systems and Supporting Techniques*—is the foundation of the present and future development of the ISO 14000 series of standards.

Environmental Management System

One model for an EMS, inspired from the practical use of the ISO 9000 standards, is presented in Figure 14-1. Executive management establishes its environmental policy, which is an integral part of the company's mission. Just like the quality policy, it can be deployed by a policy manual. The environmental requirements for processes can be implemented in procedures and work instructions, which constitute a concrete way for middle management and employees to respect the environmental requirements. Personnel will therefore find in the procedures *what to do, when to do it*, and *how to do it*. Quality plans and records for products must contain environmental requirements. Internal environmental audits ensure, in a systematic way, the operation of environmental management systems and the discovery of improvement opportunities. The results of these audits are analyzed during management reviews, when executives can compare them with their environmental policies and objectives. Internal audits, management reviews, and the resulting actions form an improvement and reinforcement cycle that empowers people and creates an environmental culture in companies. Meanwhile, the environmental system must be incorporated within the quality system. This incorporation could be confirmed by mixed certification in accordance with the requirements of ISO the 9000 and ISO 14000 standards. Finally, as shown in Figure 14-1, the environmental management system must serve, first and foremost, for the *protection of the environment*.

The compatibility between the specifications of EMS (ISO 14001: 1996) and the quality system requirements (ISO 9001: 1994) will facilitate the implementation of an EMS system by companies that already operate a quality system.

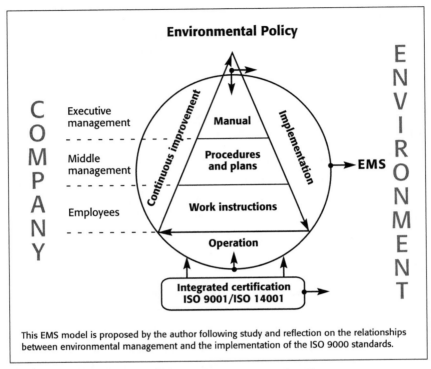

This EMS model is proposed by the author following study and reflection on the relationships between environmental management and the implementation of the ISO 9000 standards.

Figure 14-1. Environmental Management System (EMS)

In this new world it will be much easier for a company that wants to compete in global markets to connect its core processes with the core processes of its customers, suppliers, subcontractors, and distributors thanks to the models proposed by international standards.

Notes

1. International Chamber of Commerce (ICC), *Business Charter for Sustainable Development*, Section 2: Integrated Management.

2. Mark Morrow, "ISO 9000 Serves the Environment," *Quality Digest*, April 1993, p. 24.

3. Standards Council of Canada, October 1995.

4. E. Kirschner, E. Chynoweth, and L. Tattum, "Measure, Verify, Audit for Credibility," *Chemical Week*, July 7-14, 1993, p. 28-29.

15

In the Race for Prosperity

During one of my latest management seminars for service organizations, certain participating managers from Xerox, Bell Canada, Komatsu Canada, and others asked me about the future of the ISO 9000 standards. I answered: "I think that the construction of the business world during the next 10 years will be done with the active participation of ISO standardization for management systems. I predict that in 50 years companies will be using the principles of quality management in their business practices."

The ISO 9000 series is becoming increasingly interesting to enterprises, companies, and organizations throughout the world. Studies reveal that 50 percent of European companies are already registered to ISO 9000 and the phenomenon is continuing.[1] *Quality Digest* published forecasts from studies indicating that more than half a million North American companies are likely to seek ISO 9000 registration in the short term.[2]

It is important to recognize that the ISO 9000 standards constitute a universal language in the new business world. Never in world history has a standard been as popular and as widely used. Today, ISO quality system standardization has become a lever of world trade. It is a marketing tool as well as a guide for quality management, which gives companies a great number of advantages (see Figure 15-1). The implementation of ISO 9000 empowers personnel with concrete means to perform quality work, initiates the business process redesign, decreases the costs of nonquality and starts up continuous improvement. Moreover, suppliers and subcontractors are led to compare themselves with the contractual requirements of ISO and to improve their quality systems. Finally, ISO is a solid foundation from which to start up strategic business management, which seeks better results in the long term for the company and its stakeholders.

The ISO 9000 certificate is a passport for modern management, based on quality planning, quality control, quality assurance, and quality improvement. It allows companies to play in the world competitive arena. It is neither a miracle solution nor a ceiling for progress. In-house, certification becomes a milestone in the race for prosperity.

In brief, ISO provides companies with an assurance that increases their competitive edge. But, should a company stop after having implemented ISO?

First, ISO does not allow such an end, since quality systems involve continued support and improvement, and the standards themselves evolve every five years. In practice, companies that have obtained spectacular results thanks to quality—such as Xerox, Motorola, Disney, General Electric, Kodak, and Federal Express in the United States; Nortel and Bell in Canada; Toyota and Komatsu in Japan; and Rhône Poulenc, British Airways, and BMW in Europe—are continuing their quality efforts to respond to the dynamic evolution of the world market with better competitiveness, more flexibility, and greater ability to customize. These companies are convinced that their current quality of products, services, and processes is not sufficient. They adopt, improve, and rethink management approaches that link all processes in the company with a strategic multidimensional vision

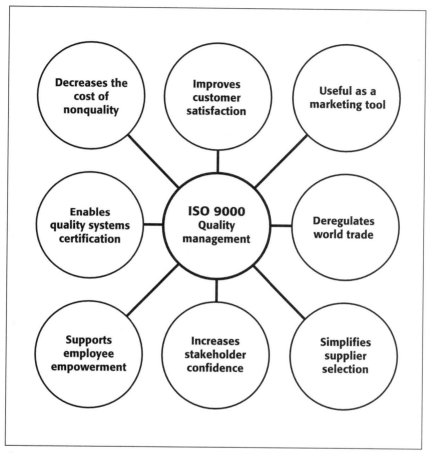

Figure 15-1. Advantages of ISO 9000

for the satisfaction of all stakeholders (owners, customers, suppliers, people, the environment, and society).

Quality is a lever of prosperity. To prosper in the future, companies will have to exceed certificates, awards, excellence programs, and even stakeholders' expectations (see Figure 15-2). As Tom Peters said, "Excellent firms don't believe in excellence—only in constant improvement and constant change."[3] Not only must they believe in change, they must also bring about change, and they must do this in accordance with a long-term vision.

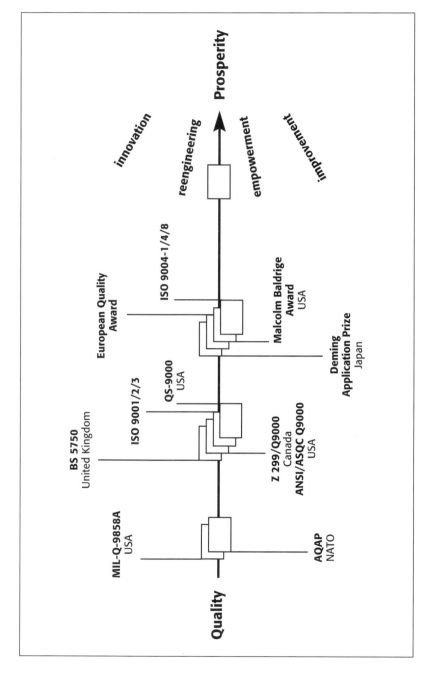

Figure 15-2. The Quality Management Continuum in the Race for Prosperity

Notes

1. K. K. Hockman, "U.S. Firms Bid to Meet European Quality Standards," *The Wall Street Journal Europe*, October 8, 1991.

2. Mark Morrow, "U.S. ISO 9000 Registrations Double," *Quality Digest*, November 1992, p. 18.

3. Tom Peters, *Thriving on Chaos*, New York: Knopf, 1987, p. 4.

16

The Nortel Case Study[1]

Nortel's Broadband Networks division in Montreal is one of the showcases of high technology in Quebec. The division designs, manufactures, and installs transmission equipment for customers in Canada, the United States, Europe, and Asia. This division has devoted much effort to the implementation and start-up of a new quality system based on the ISO 9001 standard. The goal of certification is to demonstrate, to its customers around the world, its capacity to supply high-quality products. In-house, the objective is to put in place a quality system allowing each person to better understand his or her work and to prevent errors. Implementation was started with the new FiberWorld product line because of its strategic importance for future business.

As with many new initiatives, the launching of the ISO 9001 implementation met with some resistance on the part of managers. This originated from their lack of understanding of the quality management system, and from the lack of information available regarding the certification process and the objectives sought. Certain unit managers questioned the necessity of the ISO standard; others saw it as an increase in paperwork; still others were apprehensive of the overtime work that such implementation would require.

A three-month sensitization period was necessary to convince the managers of the advantages of an ISO 9001 quality system. This sensitization was characterized by the personal commitment of the division's vice president, by informational meetings, and by communication memos. As a result, managers started to appreciate the advantages that such a quality system would offer—including executive management, quality objectives, order review, design, manufacturing, inspection, equipment, shipping, and servicing—compared with the existing verification program, which was limited to processes.

Four persons attended a specialized course on the ISO standards, and upon their return an ISO coordination committee was formed, reporting to the manufacturing department. This committee then trained all shop employees. In parallel, executive management issued a short information bulletin to employees explaining why the division was seeking ISO 9001 certification and what the implementation entailed. The ISO coordinating committee then established an action plan containing the steps to follow, the milestones, and the responsibilities. After executive management approved the general plan, each department drew up its own plan in accordance with the established schedule. Supported by executive management, the coordinating committee followed up on the schedules to avoid delays.

In February 1992 a team made up of four auditors from the registrar QMI (Quality Management Institute) performed an audit of the whole quality system. This audit took place according to audit plan and in conformance with the ISO 10011 standard. This plan included the audit's scope, the lead auditor, the auditors, the 20 ISO 9001 requirements, the audit schedule, and the audit areas. With the help of a 250-question checklist, the audit team examined the objective and scope of the quality documentation. The QMI team assessed, on-site, the implementation of the documents based on the objective evidence present. Finally, thanks to the audit's positive results, the

FiberWorld module received its ISO 9001 certification. Employee efforts in the certification were recognized and celebrated in a party.

One year after certification Nortel managers could determine the effects of the ISO 9001 quality system. The procurement director is convinced that ISO simplifies his work. He receives certificates by fax from suppliers in Japan, Singapore, Europe, the U.S., and Canada. All he has to do is ensure that the organization that issued the certificate is officially recognized. According to him, his suppliers' priorities are ISO 9001 certification and the environmental management system. During his 20 years in this business, the procurement director has never before seen such a commitment on the part of suppliers. During a February, 1993 business trip in Singapore, he was impressed to see that five newspapers were advertising the ISO 9000 certification of local companies on several pages.

According to the quality director, the ISO 9001 model allows companies to deal with personnel fluctuations without altering quality in manufacturing. He is convinced that information flow and personnel training have greatly improved. The result is a decrease in functional defects (even if the defect criteria are more stringent today than they were before ISO implementation), a reduction of nonconformities caused by ignorance, and a greater discipline in process execution. The quality director estimates, in his experience, that the management model proposed by the ISO standards permitted a tripling in production capacity without increasing the number of senior managers. The manager/employee ratio has hence decreased as a result of the establishment of autonomous work teams and greater responsibility given to employees. Hence, by empowering the personnel, senior management is relieved of the management of daily activities and can concentrate on strategic management of the division.

One member of the division's ISO coordination committee summarizes the management process in this way: "ISO makes us do what we should do." He finds the effects of the quality system on the personnel very significant. The employees now have at their disposal concrete tools (training, work instructions, forms, etc.) to perform quality work. They transmit their suggestions on a simple form and an independent team of engineers examines each proposal and takes appropriate action. The ISO coordinator estimates that the recording and follow-up of corrective actions has also been improved. In fact, eliminating root causes of problems allows the continuous improvement of processes, which reduces the quantity and severity of problems.

According to one of the manufacturing managers, the amount of repair and rework of circuit boards during assembly has noticeably decreased. In his mind, even if the procedures were excellent before implementation of the quality system, it is this system that ensures their application. He also asserts that standardization is a tool that leads to continous improvement, and to a philosophy centered on quality that translates into discipline in process execution.

Two years after certification Nortel can discern a relationship between the empowerment of personnel, external and internal quality audits, and the maturity of the quality system. As Figure 16-1 illustrates, maintaining a steady increase in employee motivation is not an easy task. Thanks to the internal audits performed by the quality department and the external audits conducted by the registrar and customers, the effective running of the quality system is always ensured.

Implementation of the ISO 9001 standard supports Nortel's other initiatives, such as the "Excellence" continuous improvement program and Environmental Management System. ISO 9001 allows the division to take one more step toward prosperity. Product line revenues increased in 1994 to $2.47 billion (28 percent of total) from $2.22 billion (27 percent of total) in 1993 and $2.11 billion (25 percent of total) in 1992. The quality system support increase was due to higher demand, especially in the United States and Europe.[2]

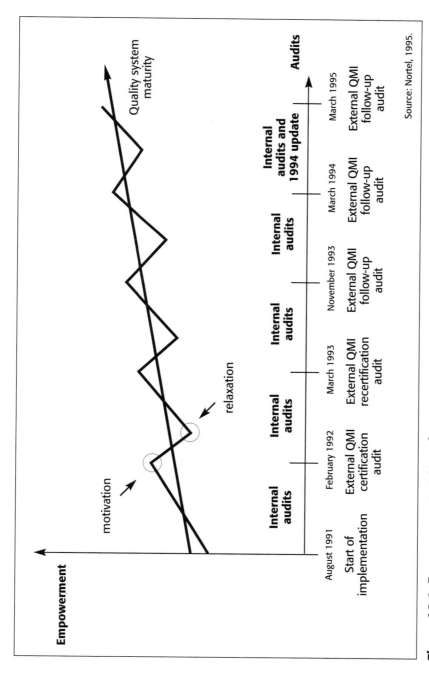

Figure 16-1. Empowerment at Nortel

Notes

1. Case written with the authorization of Northern Telecom Canada Limited, May 1993 and 1995.

2. Nortel, *A World of Networks* (1994 Annual Report), 1995, p. 43.

Bibliography

"A Quick Review." *Purchasing* 114, no. 1 (14 January 1993): 76.

Albrecht, Karl, and Ron Zemke. *Service America!* Homewood, Ill.: Dow Jones Irwin, 1985.

Arter, Dennis R. "Demystifying the ISO 9000/Q90 Series Standards." *Quality Progress* 25, no. 11 (November 1992): 65-67.

Aschner, Gabor S. "ISO 9000 as Your Competitive Edge." *Journal for Quality & Participation* 15, no. 5 (September 1992): 50-53.

AT&T Corporate Quality Office, "Using ISO 9000 to Improve Business Processes." AT&T Customer Information Center, Indianapolis.

Avery, Susan. "Where Does ISO 9000 Fit?" *Purchasing* 114, no. 1 (14 January 1993): 75-77.

"BAI First Architects in North America to Be Registered to ISO 9001." *QMI Brief,* April 1994.

Benson, Tracy E. "Quality Goes International." *Industry Week* 240, no. 16 (19 August 1991): 54-57.

Berkman, Barbara N. "Why Europe Needs a Common European Standard." *Electronic Business* 16, no. 19 (15 October 1990): 189-190.

Berthelot, Ron. "Making the Most of ISO 9000." *Training & Development* 47, no. 2 (February 1993): 9.

Bertin, Patrick. "Le coût d'obtention de la qualité." *Informations Chimie* no. 325 (January-February 1991): 167-70.

Bishara, R., and M. Wyrick. "A Systematic Approach to Quality Assurance Auditing." *Quality Progress* 27, no. 12 (December 1994): 73-77.

Blumberg, Donald F. "Field Service Quality Improves with Technology: Experience at Frontier Refreshment Services." *National Productivity Review* 11, no. 1 (January 1992): 87-96.

Bodinson, Glenn W. "Warning: Ignoring ISO Standards May Be Harmful to Your Company's Future." *Industrial Management* 33, no. 2 (March/April 1991): 11-12.

Boehling, Walter H. "Europe 1992 : Its Effect on International Standards." *Quality Progress* 23, no. 6 (June 1990): 29-32.

Borthick, A. Faye, and Harold P. Roth. "Will Europeans Buy Your Company's Products?" *Business Credit* 94, no. 10 (Nov/Dec 1992): 23-24.

Borthick, A. Faye, and Harold P. Roth. "Will Europeans Buy Your Company's Products?" *Management Accounting* 74, no. 1 (July 1992): 28-32.

Bowen, Robert. "ISO 9000: The Foundation of a Long-Term Continuous Improvement Strategy." *ISO 9000 News* 1, no. 3 (May 1992): 10.

Bowman, Robert. "The State of Quality in Logistics—Allied-Signal; Hoechst Celanese; Olin Corp.; Subaru of America; Union Camp." *Distribution* 91, no. 8 (August 1992): 90-96.

Boznak, Rudolf, G. "Manufacturers Must Prepare for International Quality Initiative." *Industrial Engineering* 23, no. 10 (October 1991): 13-14.

Brecka, Jon. "QS-9000 Activities Heating Up." *Quality Progress* (April 1995): 20.

Brumm, Eugenia K. "Managing Records for ISO 9000 Compliance." *Quality Progress* 28, no. 1 (January 1995): 73-77.

Bureau of Business Practice, *ISO 9000: Handbook of Quality Standards and Compliance*. Milwaukee: Quality Press, 1992.

Burr, John T. "The Future Necessity." *Quality Progress* 23, no. 6 (June 1990): 17-23.

Burrows, Peter. "Behind the Facade of ISO 9000." *Electronic Business* 18, no. 2 (27 January 1992): 40-44.

Byrnes, Daniel. "Exploring the World of ISO 9000." *Quality* 31, no. 10 (October 1992): 19-31.

CAN P-10. *Criteria and Procedures for Accreditation of Organizations Registering Quality Systems.* 1991.

Cartwright, Graham. "Lessons Learned about ISO 9000." *Journal for Quality & Participation* 15, no. 5 (September 1992): 44-48.

Chynoweth, Emma and Rick Mullin. "ISO 9000: Providing the Basis for Quality—Industry Cleaves to an International Standard." *Chemical Week* 150, no. 17 (29 April 1992): 30-31.

Chynoweth, Emma, and Karen Heller. "Wanted: A System to Audit Care." *Chemical Week* 150, no. 23 (17 June, 1992): 28-32.

Chynoweth, Emma. "Health/Safety Model: ISO 9000."*Chemical Week* 151, no. 12 (30 September, 1992): 62.

Chynoweth, Emma. "ISO 9000: International Community Continues Talks on Mutual Recognition." *Chemical Week* 151, no. 19 (Nov 11, 1992): 40-46.

Cook, Brian M. "Global Competition—The European Way." *Industry Week* 241, no. 13 (6 July 1992): 64.

Cornick, T.C., and N.J. Bare. "Quality Management and Design-Build: The Opportunities for This Method of Procurement." *International Journal of Quality and Reliability Management* 6, no. 3 (1991): 17-20.

Corrigan, James. "Is ISO 9000 the Path to TQM?" *Quality Progress* 27, no. 5 (May 1994): 33-36.

Costanzo, Anthony. "US Corporate Executive Knowledge of ISO 9000 Lacking." *Quality* 31, no. 9 (September 1992): 47-48.

Cottman, Ronald J., *A Guidebook to ISO 9000 and ANSI/ASQC Q90,* Milwaukee: Quality Press, 1993.

"Criteria Set for Those Wishing to Serve as Third-Party Registrars for QS-9000." *Quality Progress* (March 1995): 21.

Crosby, Philip. *Quality without Tears.* New York: Plume/New American Library, 1984.

Crystal, Charlotte. "A Weak Commitment to Managing Quality." *International Business* 7, no. 7, July 1994, p. 20.

Crystal, Charlotte. "Your Quality Passport to European Sales." *International Business* 5, no. 9 (September 1992): 74-75.

CSA. *Focus* 4, no. 3 (special quality issue, 1990): 3.

Curley, Jeffrey P. "Quality Systems Manual Method." *Quality Digest* (April 1993): 68-72.

Dambrot, Stuart. "No Easy Path Seen at Tokyo: Forum Cites Obstacles to Be Overcome." *Chemical Week*, 150, no. 17 (29 April 1992): 48.

Davis, Stanley. *Future Perfect*. Reading, Mass.: Addison-Wesley, 1987.

DeAngelis, Cynthia A. "ICI Advanced Materials Implements ISO 9000 Program." *Quality Progress* 24, no. 11 (November 1991): 49-51.

Deming, W. Edwards. *Out of the Crisis*. Cambridge, Mass.: MIT Center for Advanced Engineering Studies, 1986.

Dubashi, Jagannath. "Sheepskin: Why Caterpillar, Trinova and Northen Telecom Fight to Get This Certificate." *Financial World* 162 (13 April 1993): 66-67.

Durand, Ian G., Donald W. Marquard, Robert W. Peach, and James C. Pyle. "Updating the ISO 9000 Quality Standards: Responding to Marketplace Needs." *Quality Progress* 26, no. 7 (July 1993): 23-28.

Dutton, Barbara. "Quality in the Glen." *Manufacturing Systems* 10, no. 3 (March 1992): 20-26.

Dzus, George. "Planning a Successful ISO 9000 Assessment." *Quality Progress* 24, no. 11 (November 1991): 43-46.

Emmons, Sidney L. "Value-Added Audit Training." *Quality Progress* 27, no. 5 (May 1994): 45-47.

EN 45012. *General Criteria for Certification Bodies Operating Quality System Certification*.

"Exporting Pays Off." *Business America* 114 (22 March 1993): 20-21.

Federal Express. "FedEx to Receive the First System-wide ISO 9001 Certification." *FedEx Fact Sheet*, September 15, 1994.

Ferguson, Kelly H. "International Quality Standards May Affect Industry's Efforts in Europe." *Pulp & Paper* 65, no. 3 (March 1991): 59-62.

Ferguson, Kelly H. "Westvaco Covington Mill First in U.S. to Attain Certification Under ISO 9002." *Pulp & Paper* 66, no. 2 (February 1992): 76-81.

Fiorentino, R., and M. Perigord. "Going from an Investigative to a Formative Auditor." *Quality Progress* 28, no. 10 (November 1995): 61-65.

Flister, John D., and Joseph J. Jozaitis. "PPG's Journey to ISO 9000: Certification Is Critical to Becoming a World-Class Supplier." *Management Accounting* 74, no. 1 (July 1992): 33-38.

"Focus on Quality." *Manufacturing Engineering* 109 (5 (November 1992): 17.

Forbes, Lincoln H. "Achieving Professional Success in a Decade of Economic Uncertainty." *Industrial Engineering* 24, no. 9 (September 1992): 58-63.

Fouhy, Ken, Gulam Samdani, and Stephen Moore. "ISO 9000: A New Road to Quality." *Chemical Engineering* 99, no. 10 (October 1992): 43-47.

Freese, Jesse D., and Emily Konold. "Teamwork Pays Off for Firm." *Quality Progress* 27, no. 5 (May 1994): 53-55.

Genevray, Robert. "Un système d'assurance de la qualité: est-ce une nécessité pour tous?" *Qualité* 17 (October/November 1990): 50-57.

Gooley, Toby B. "Your Roadmap to ISO 9000." *Traffic Management* 32 (February 1993): 49-54.

Gorman, Doug. "Beyond ISO 9000 Certification: A Better Reason for Documenting Your Quality System." *Quality Digest* (December 1992): 47-50.

Graham, John F. "Texas Petrochemical Plant Gets Certification." *Oil & Gas Journal* 89, no. 19 (13 May 1991): 48-50.

Greene, Alice H. "ISO 9000 : Globalizing Quality Standards." *Production & Inventory Management* 11, no. 9 (September 1991): 12-15.

Greising, David. "Quality How to Make It Pay." *Business Week*, August 8, 1994: 54-59.

Grossi, Giovanni. "Quality Certifications." *Internal Auditor*, 49, no. 5 (October 1992): 33-35.

Guyard, Cristian. "L'irrésistible ascension de la certification." *Industries et Techniques* no. 724 (April 10, 1992): 42-47.

Haderer, Ed. "Setting Tough Standards." *China Business Review* 20 (January/February 1993): 34-36.

Hagigh, Sara E. "Obtaining EC Product Approvals After 1992: What American Manufacturers Need to Know." *Business America* 113, no. 4 (24 February 1992): 30-33.

Halligan, Beate. "ISO 9000 Standards Prepare You to Compete." *Industrial Distribution* 81, no. 6 (May/June 1992): 100.

Hamilton, William R. "How to Construct a Basic Quality Manual." *Quality Progress* 28, no. 4 (April 1995): 71-73.

Harrewijn, Jo. "What Will ISO 9000 Standards Bring Us . . . A New Bureaucracy or a Living Quality System?" *Journal for Quality & Participation* 14, no. 4 (July/August 1991): 22-26.

Heap, John. "Quality and BS 5750." *Management Services* (UK) 35, no. 3 (March 1991): 22-23.

Heller, Karen. "Compliance Benefits Staff at Ethyl: Understanding of Operations Is Enhanced." *Chemical Week*, 150, no. 17 (29 April 1992): 52.

Heller, Karen. "Stepping-Stone on the Road to a Global Economy." *Chemical Week* 152, no. 5 (10 February, 1993: 30-32.

Heller, Karen. "Tying It All Together—With or without ISO 9000." *Chemical Week* 152, no. 5 (10 February 1993): 31.

Hendry, Ian. "World Quality Guide: ISO 9000 Standardizes Paper Quality Efforts." *Pulp & Paper* 67, no. 1 (January 1993): SS3-SS39.

Henkoff, Ronald. "The Hot New Seal of Quality." *Fortune*, 28 June 1993, 116-120.

Henkoff, Ronald. "Service Is Everybody's Business." *Fortune*, 27 June 1994, 49.

Hockman, Kymberly K. "Taking the Mystery Out of Quality." *Training & Development* 46, no. 7 (July 1992): 34-39.

Hockman, Kymberly K. "U.S. Firms Bid to Meet European Quality Standards." *The Wall Street Journal Europe*, 8 October 1991.

Hokman, Kimberly K. "Road Map to ISO 9000 Registration." *Quality Progress*, 27, no. 5 (May 1994): 39-42.

"Hyundai Heavy Industries: Moving Up the Technology Ladder." *Business Korea* 10 (January 1993): 63.

Industry Canada. *Entry Guide for the Canada Awards for Excellence.* 1995.

"Informex Is Network Center for Custom Manufacturers." *Chemical Marketing Reporter* 243, no. 7 (15 February, 1993 p. 5, 26.

Inglesby, Tom. "An Interview with Tracy O'Rourke." *Manufacturing Systems* 9, no. 11 (November 1991): 22-29.

Inglesby, Tom. "ISO 9002 : The Exeter Story." *Manufacturing Systems* 10, no. 1 (January 1992): 27-31.

Ingman, Lars C. "Buying Right: Pushing Quality Upstream." *Pulp & Paper* 65, no. 4 (April 1991): 175-177.

Ingman, Lars C. "Quality Systems." *Pulp & Paper* 65, no. 1 (January 1991): 137-139.

Ingman, Lars C. "Testing, Measurement, and Inspection." *Pulp & Paper* 65, no. 6 (June 1991): 131-133.

Ingman, Lars C. "The Quality Audit." *Pulp & Paper* 65, no. 10 (October 1991): 125-127.

Ingman, Lars C. "Product Tracking and Process Control." *Pulp & Paper* 65, no. 5 (May 1991): 155-157.

International Chamber of Commerce (ICC). *Business Charter for Sustainable Development*, Section 2: Integrated Management.

"Interview: Bernard Fournier, Rank Xerox." *Quality Link* 4, no. 21 (December 1992): 5.

"ISEA Communique." *Occupational Hazards* 54, no. 1 (January 1992): 53-54.

ISO, *ISO 9000 Compendium*, 5th ed., 1995.

"ISO/IEC Mulls Over Decision to Adopt Proposal." *Quality Progress* (September 1994): 22.

"ISO 9000: Making Quality the Standard for Canadian Suppliers." *The Supplier* no. 13 (Spring 1993): 6.

Jackson, Suzan L. "What You Should Know About ISO 9000." *Training* 29, no. 5 (May/June 1992): 48-52.

Jasany, Leslie C. "PLCs: Focusing on Integration." *Automation* 38, no. 4 (April 1991): 28-36.

Jedd, Marcia. "ISO 9000 or BUST." *Distribution* 92 (February 1993): 39-44.

Johnston, Cristopher E. "Stan Salot Credits ISO 9000 as the Basis for Logitech's Successful Quality-Improvement Efforts." *Quality Digest* (September 1992): 29-36.

Juran, Joseph. "Made in U.S.A.: A Renaissance in Quality." *Harvard Business Review* (July-August 1993): 47.

Juran, Joseph, and Frank Gryna. *Juran's Quality Control Handbook*, 4th ed. New York: McGraw-Hill, 1988.

Kagan, Andrew. "ISO 9000: Transport Engineering Sectors Move Toward Registration." *Chemical Week* 151, no. 19 (11 November 1992): 48-52.

Kalinosky, Ian S. "The Total Quality System—Going Beyond ISO 9000." *Quality Progress* 23, no. 6 (June 1990): 50-54.

Kelly, Kevin. "A Bean-Counter's Best Friend." *Business Week* (special quality issue, January 1992): 42-43.

Kemezis, Paul. "Confusion Persists on Issue of Registrar Accreditation." *Chemical Week* (28 April 1993): 42.

Kemezis, Paul. "Du Pont, Eastman Lead in the U.S.: Head Start from Europe." *Chemical Week* 150, no. 17 (29 April 1992): 49-50.

Kemezis, Paul. "Europe-Based Firms Exporting ISO 9000." *Chemical Week* 151, no. 19 (11 November, 1992): 57.

Kendrick, John J. "Certifying Quality Management Systems." *Quality* 29, no. 8 (August 1990): 38-40.

Kirschner, Elisabeth, and Ronald Begley. "ISO 9000—ISP: A Variety of Challenges; Hercules Finds." *Chemical Week* 151, no. 19 (11 November, 1992): 56-57.

Kirschner, Elisabeth, ands Rick Mullin. "ISO 9000—Union Carbide: A Metamorphosis; Elf Atochem: Sets U.S. Schedule." *Chemical Week* 151, no. 19 (November 1992): 54-55.

Kirschner, Elisabeth, Emma Chynoweth, and Lyn Tattum. "Measure, Verify, Audit for Credibility." *Chemical Week* (7-14 July 1993): 28-29.

Klock, Joseph J. "How to Manage 3,500 (or Fewer) Suppliers." *Quality Progress* 23, no. 6 (June 1990): 43-47.

"Kodak Canada." *La Presse* (Montreal), March 20, 1993.

Kume Hitoshi. "Les normes ISO 9000 et leur mise en application." *ISO Bulletin* 23, no. 8 (August 1992): 4.

Kume Hitoshi. "Le point de vue japonais sur les normes ISO 9000." *Qualité en mouvement* no. 8 (November 1992): 48-50.

Lamprecht, James L. "ISO 9000 Implementation Strategies." *Quality* 30, no. 11 (November 1991): 14-17.

Lamprecht, James. "Qualité à la française." *Quality Progress* 26, no. 6 (June 1993): 31-35.

Larson, Melissa. "ISO 9000: Fad or Foundation?" *Packaging* 37, no. 8 (July 1992): 46.

Laucis, Peter K. "1993 to Focus on Quality and the Environment." *Adhesives Age* 36, no. 1 (14 January 1993 p. 26-29.

Layman, Patricia. "Du Pont Sets Venture to Market Quality Systems." *Chemical & Engineering News* 71, no. 5 (1 February 1993): 18-21.

Leeuwenburgh, Todd. "Quality Standards That Can Open Doors." *Nation's Business* 80, no. 11 (November 1992): 32-33.

Levine, Jonathan B. "Want EC Business? You Have Two Choices." *Business Week*, 19 October 1992, 58-59.

Lindsay, Karen F. "ISO 9000 Standard Spreads to U.S.—and to U.S. Processors." *Modern Plastics* 69, no. 10 (October 1992): 72-73.

Lindsay, Karen F. "Two Molders See ISO 9000 Listing as Key to Competing Globally." *Modern Plastics* 69, no. 8 (August 1992): 20-21.

Locke, John W. "Quality Standards for Laboratories." *Quality Progress* 26, no. 7 (July 1993).

Lofgren, George Q. "Quality System Registration." *Quality Progress* 24, no. 5 (May 1991): 35-37.

Luc, Danielle, and Branimir Todorov. "In Search of World-Class Suppliers." Groupe de concertation sur la qualité, Montreal, September 1992.

Marash, Stanley A., and Donald W. Marquard. "Quality, Standards, and Free Trade." *Quality Progress* 27, no. 5 (May 1994): 27-30.

Marquardt, D., J. Chové, K. E. Jensen, K. Petrick, J. Pyle, and D. Strahle. "Vision 2000: The Strategy for the ISO 9000 Series Standards in the 90s." *Quality Progress* 24, no. 5 (May 1991): 25-31.

Marquardt, Donald W. "ISO 9000: A Universal Standard of Quality." *Management Review* 81, no. 1 (January 1992): 50-52.

McDermott, Kevin. "When Quality Becomes a Trade Barrier." *D&B Reports* 40, no. 3 (May/June 1992).

McFadyen, Tunney, and Tim Walsh. "Is ISO 9000 Worth the Paper It's Written On?" *Journal for Quality & Participation* 15, no. 2 (March 1992): 20-23.

McGovern, John P. "Quality: The Spirit of Europe." *Journal for Quality & Participation* 14, no. 4 (July/August 1991): 18-20.

Miller, Cyndee. "ISO Status Not Only for Big Firms." *Marketing News* 27, no. 4 (15 February 1993): 6.

Miller, Cyndee. "U.S. Firms Lag in Meeting Global Quality Standards." *Marketing News* 27, no. 4 (15 February 1993): 1-6.

Mitonneau, Henri. *Reussir l'audit qualité*. Paris: AFNOR, 1988.

Morris, Gregory DL. "Responsible Care—Distribution: Assuring Safe Handling over Land, Sea, and Air." *Chemical Week* 148, no. 26 (17 July 1991): 18-24.

Morrow, Mark. "Geneva Summit Targets Harmony." *Chemical Week*, 28 April 1993): 43, 46.

Morrow, Mark. "ISO 9000 Serves the Environment." *Quality Digest* (April 1993): 24.

Morrow, Mark. "The Steady March of ISO 9000." *Quality Digest* (May 1993): 22.

Morrow, Mark. "U.S. ISO 9000 Registrations Double." *Quality Digest* (November 1992): 18.

Mullin, Rick, and Elisabeth S. Kieshe, "Life After Registration: Are We There Yet?" *Chemical Week* (28 April 1993): 34 - 40.

Mullin, Rick, and Paul Kemezis. "ISO 9000: Hoechst Targets Full Registration; Dow Starts Its U.S. Program." *Chemical Week* 151, no. 19 (11 November 1992): 52-53.

Mullin, Rick. "Building a U.S. Infrastructure: Chemical Sector Full Speed Ahead." *Chemical Week* 150, no. 17 (29 April 1992): 31-32.

Mullin, Rick. "Commitment and Corporate Culture: Management's New Mechanism." *Chemical Week* 150, no. 17 (29 April 1992): 42-45.

Mullin, Rick. "Maintenance Software: The Next Generation." *Chemical Week* 151, no. 8 (26 August 1992): 33-34.

Mullin, Rick. "Service Sector Gets in Line: Still No Rush to Register." *Chemical Week* 150, no. 17 (29 April 1992): 46.

Naisbitt, John. *Global Paradox*. New York: Avon Books, 1995.

Naisbitt, John, and Patricia Aburdene. *Megatrends 2000*. New York: Avon Books, 1991.

Nelms, Douglas W. "British Airways Brands a New Image." *Air Transport World* 30 (January 1993): 70-71

Ness, J. A., and T. G. Cucuzza. "Tapping the Full Potential of ABC." *Harvard Business Review*, July/August 1995: 130-138.

Niese, Ann. "Standard Supports U.S., Foreign Markets." *Computer Technology Review* 12, no. 11 (September 1992): 14.

Noaker, Paula M. "Down the Road with DNC." *Manufacturing Engineering* 109, no. 5 (November 1992): 35-38.

"Les normes internationales, une clé pour l'ouverture des marchés." *ISO Bulletin* 23, no. 10 (October 1992): 3.

Peach, R. "ISO 9000 Series, Quality Management and Quality Assurance." *Annual Quality Congress Transactions*, San Francisco, CA, ASQC, 14-16 May 1990, 968-974.

Pechter, Kerry. "Benelux: In Europe's Epicenter . . . ." *International Business* 5, no. 8 (August 1992): 44-49.

Perna, Frank, Jr., D. Munson, J. Robertson, C. Kroll, Fred F. Campagna, and Michael J. Gambino. "Industry Leaders Assess the Impact of EC '92." *Consulting-Specifying Engineer* 10, no. 7 (December 1991): 58-64.

Peters, Tom. *Thriving on Chaos*. New York: Knopf, 1987.

Pfeifer, Charles G. and Alfred H. Strolle. "Du Pont's Quality Improvement Steward." *Quality* 31, no. 8 (August 1992): Q26-Q27.

Pirret, Rick. "Automated Calibration for ISO 9000; What's the Difference?" *Quality* 31, no. 11 (November 1992): 15-19.

Placek, Chester. "Baldrige Award as a Quality Model." *Quality* 31, no. 2 (February 1992): 17-20.

Plishner, Emily S. "ISO 9000—Air Products: A Multisite Approach." *Chemical Week* 151, no. 19 (11 November 1992): 56.

Plishner, Emily S. "ISO 9000—Seeking Recognition: U.S. Auditors Build Their Base." *Chemical Week* 151, no. 19 (11 November 1992): 30-32.

Plishner, Emily S. "Latin America Installing Registration Infrastructure." *Chemical Week* (April 1993): 52.

Plishner, Emily S. "ISO 9000—Witco's Certification Plan: Total Immersion." *Chemical Week* 151, no. 19 (11 November 1992): 54.

Plug, Bryan. "Bringing Quality to Accounting." *CMA Magazine* (July-August 1992): 17-19.

Quality Management Institute, *The Corporate Quality Guide*. Mississauga, Ontario: QMI, 1992.

Quality Management Institute, "The QMI Registration Program." 1994.

Ray L. Robinson. "Professional Profile: USS—Ray L. Robinson." *Purchasing* 113, no. 7 (11 November 1992): 49.

Rayner, P., and L.J. Porter. "BS5750/ISO9000—The Experience of Small and Medium-Sized Firms." *International Journal of Quality and Reliability Management* 8, no. 6 (1991): 16-28.

Remich, Norman C., Jr. "Standards: The Foundation for Global Commerce." *Appliance Manufacturer* 40, no. 10 (October 1992): 82-86.

Rice, Craig M. " How to Conduct an Internal Quality Audit and Still Have Friends." *Quality Progress* 27, no. 6 (June 1994): 39-41

Roberts, Michael. "Responsible Care: Rotterdam." *Chemical Week* 150, no. 23 (17 June 1992): 144.

Rock, Matthew. "Twists and Turns on Quality Street." *Director* 46, no. 5 (December 1992): 40-43.

Rogers, Larry. "Certification du système qualité en Amérique du Nord." *Colloque: La certification des entreprises*, Paris, January 8, 1991.

Russell, J.P. "Quality Management Benchmark Assessment." *Quality Progress* 28, no. 5, (May 1995): 57-61.

Sakofsky, Steven. "Survival After ISO 9000 Registration." *Quality Progress* 27, no. 5 (May 1994): 57-59.

Sateesh, Kris. "ISO 9000 Sets the Stage for Global Competition."*Controls & Systems* 39, no. 9 (September 1992): 22-24.

Saunders, Mary. "ISO 9000 and Marketing in Europe: Should U.S. Manufacturers Be Concerned?" *Business America* 113, no. 8 (20 April 1992): 24-25.

Sawin, Stephen D. "Selecting an ISO 9000 Registrar." *Quality* 31, no. 8 (August 1992): Q24-Q25.

Schindler, Gene, and James Lamprecht. "E & P Companies, Suppliers Move to International Standards." *Oil & Gas Journal* 89, no. 18 (6 May 1991): 92-98.

Schnoll, Les. "One World, One Standard." *Quality Progress* (April 1993): 35-39.

Shaughnessy, R.N. "La normalisation au cours des années 1990, un enjeu vers une amélioration radicale." *Consensus* (hiver 1992): 27-29.

Shaughnessy, R.N. "La transition de nationales à globales des normes de qualité." *Consensus* (été 1991): 21-22.

Shaugnhessy, R.N. "Débat sur l'avenir de la série ISO 9000." *ISO 9000 News* no. 2 (July/August 1995): 1-4.

Sherman, Stratford. "Are You as Good as the Best in the World?" *Fortune*, December 3, 1993, 95.

Shingo Shigeo. *The Sayings of Shigeo Shingo: Key Strategies for Plant Improvement.* Portland, Ore.: Productivity Press, 1987.

Short, Herb. "Quality Assurance, European Style." *Chemical Engineering* 95, no. 14 (10 October 1988): 26-28.

Singleton, Stephan C. "Focus on Kodak's ISO 9000 Experience." *ISO 9000 News* no. 2, (March/April 1995): 8-11.

Slovick, Murray. "Hong Kong's Push into High Tech." *Dealerscope Merchandising* 33, no. 2 (February 1991): 43.

Smock, Doug. "Precise Plastics Targets Special Niches for Growth." *Plastics World* 50, no. 13 (December 1992): 112-113.

Socolovsky, Alberto. "Contract Manufacturing Looks to Higher Quality, Lower Costs." *Electronic Business*, 18, no. 11 (August 1992): 105-116.

Somerset, Kerry. "Phase 2 Revisions and Needs of Small Businesses." *ISO 9000 News* no. 2 (July/August 1994): 1-4.

Spickernell, D.G. "La voie vers l'ISO 9000." *ISO 9000 News* no. 1, 1992.

Spizizen, Gary. "The ISO 9000 Standards: Creating a Level Playing Field for International Quality." *National Productivity Review* 11, no. 3 (March 1992): 331-346.

Sprow, Eugene. "Insights into ISO 9000." *Manufacturing Engineering* 109, no. 3 (September 1992): 73-77.

Stern, Gary M. "Sailing to Europa: Can Auditing Play a Role in the New International Quality Standards?" *Internal Auditor* 49, no. 5 (October 1992): 29-32.

Stratton, Brad. "How Disneyland Works." *Quality Progress* (July 1991): 25-27.

Stratton, John H. "What Is the Registrar Accreditation Board?" *Quality Progress* 25, no. 1 (January 1992): 67-69.

Tattum, Lyn, and K. Heller. "An International Hallmark of Quality." *Chemical Week* 149, no. 8 (25 September 1991): 56.

Tattum, Lyn. "ISO 9000 in Europe: The Competitive Edge Is Dulled." *Chemical Week* 151, no. 19 (11 November 1992): 37-38.

Thayer, Ann M. "Value of Global Standards Becomes Clear to Chemical Industry."*Chemical & Engineering News* 71 (1 March 1993): 12-17.

Timbers, M.J. "ISO 9000 and Europe's Attempts to Mandate Quality." *Quality Digest* (June 1992): 18-30.

Tingey, Michael O. "Comparing ISO 9000, Malcolm Baldrige Award and SEI CMM criteria." *ISO 9000 News* no. 2 (March/April 1995): 22-25.

Todorov, B. "Documentation de la qualité"(course notes) Paris: IGS, 1992.

U.S. Department of Commerce. *Delivering Results: A Progress Report from the NIST.* June 1995.

U.S. Department of Commerce. *Malcolm Baldrige National Quality Award.* 1995.

U.S. Department of Defense. MIL-Q-9858A.

Van Nuland, Yves. "Prerequisites to Implementation." *Quality Progress* 23, no. 6 (June 1990): 36-39.

Van Nuland, Yves. "The New Common Language for 12 Countries." *Quality Progress* 23, no. 6 (June 1990): 40-41.

Vasilash, Gary S. "The U.S. Interface with the EEC." *Production* 103, no. 9 (September 1991): 44.

Vermeer, Frederik J. G. "ISO Certification Pays Off in Quality Improvement." *Oil & Gas Journal* 90, no. 15 (13 April 1992): 47-52.

Westwood, G. A., and B.G. Dale. "Product Liability: Implications for the Brewing Industry." *British Food Journal* 95 (1993): 18-25.

"Where in the World Is ISO 9000?" *Quality Digest* (September 1992): 22-23.

Wilson, Aubrey. "Pro-Active Stance Vital to Winning JIT Contracts." *Business Marketing Digest* 16, no. 4 (1991): 26-30.

Witt, Clyde E. "ISO 9000: A Road Map for World-Class Manufacturing; How Square D Does It." *Material Handling Engineering* 48, no. 1 (January 1993): 49-54.

Woerner, Susan. "Tools for Quality Management: ISO 9000 and Baldrige Award." *Adhesives Age* 34, no. 13 (December 1991): 41-43.

Wood, Andrew. "Going Beyond Regulations: Integrating Responsible Care with the New OSHA Rules." *Chemical Week* 150, no. 23 (17 June 1992): 44-50.

Wood, Andrew. "Responsible Care: Akzo Chemicals." *Chemical Week* 150, no. 23 (17 June 1992): 116-118.

About the Author

Branimir Todorov is president of Branimir Todorov & Associates, Inc., a quality management consulting and training company located in Montreal. He is an international quality expert, an author of management seminars, and a prominent lecturer and speaker. Mr. Todorov is a Quality Management Institute (QMI) certified auditor and an active member of several professional associations, including the American Society for Quality Control and the ISO 9000 Forum. He is the developer of a new system for the assessment of processes in the automotive industry, of an ISO 9001 audit questionnaire for manufacturing companies, and of a new system for the measurment of quality in service organizations, based on the ISO 9004-2 guidelines.

Mr. Todorov received a higher level diploma in Quality Management from the Institut de Gestion Sociale in Paris and a Master's degree in Mechanical Engineering from the Sofia University of Technology. He has taught in the MBA program of the University of Montreal Business School and the Executive MBA program of the University of Sherbrooke. Mr. Todorov has led many organizations in successfully achieving the implementation of ISO 9000 quality systems.

Index

Note: All references to illustrations are in italics.

Books from Productivity Press

Productivity Press publishes books that empower individuals and companies to achieve excellence in quality, productivity, and the creative involvement of all employees. Through steadfast efforts to support the vision and strategy of continuous improvement, Productivity Press delivers today's leading-edge tools and techniques gathered directly from industrial leaders around the world.

Call toll-free 1-800-394-6868 for our free catalog.

Learning Organizations
Developing Cultures for Tomorrow's Workplace
Sarita Chawla and John Renesch, Editors

The ability to learn faster than your competition may be the only sustainable competitive advantage! A learning organization is one where people continually expand their capacity to create results they truly desire, where new and expansive patterns of thinking are nurtured, where collective aspiration is set free, and where people are continually learning how to learn together. This compilation of 34 powerful essays, written by recognized experts worldwide, is rich in concept and theory as well as application and example. An inspiring follow-up to Peter Senge's ground-breaking best-seller *The Fifth Discipline*, these essays are grouped in four sections that address all aspects of learning organizations: the guiding ideas behind systems thinking; the theories, methods, and processes for creating a learning organization; the infrastructure of the learning model; and arenas of practice.

ISBN 1-56327-110-9 / 575 pages / $35.00 / Order LEARN-B261

Productivity Press, Inc., Dept. BK, P.O. Box 13390, Portland, OR 97213-0390
Telephone: 1-800-394-6868   Fax: 1-800-394-6286

REVISED!

20 Keys to Workplace Improvement

Iwao Kobayashi

The 20 Keys system does more than just bring together twenty of the world's top manufacturing improvement approaches—it integrates these individual methods into a closely interrelated system for revolutionizing every aspect of your manufacturing organization. This revised edition of Kobayashi's best-seller amplifies the synergistic power of raising the levels of all these critical areas simultaneously. The new edition presents upgraded criteria for the five-level scoring system in most of the 20 Keys, supporting your progress toward becoming not only best in your industry but best in the world. New material and an updated layout throughout assist managers in implementing this comprehensive approach. In addition, valuable case studies describe how Morioka Seiko (Japan) advanced in Key 18 (use of microprocessors) and how Windfall Products (Pennsylvania) adapted the 20 Keys to its situation with good results.

ISBN 1-56327-109-5/ 312 pages / $50.00 / Order 20KREV-B261

Handbook for Productivity Measurement and Improvement

William F. Christopher and Carl G. Thor, eds.

An unparalleled resource! In over 100 chapters, nearly 80 front-runners in the quality movement reveal the evolving theory and specific practices of world class organizations. Spanning a wide variety of industries and business sectors, they discuss quality and productivity in manufacturing, service industries, profit centers, administration, nonprofit and government institutions, health care and education. Contributors include Robert C. Camp, Peter F. Drucker, Jay W. Forrester, Joseph M. Juran, Robert S. Kaplan, John W. Kendrick, Yasuhiro Monden, and Lester C. Thurow. Comprehensive in scope and organized for easy reference, this compendium belongs in every company and academic institution concerned with business and industrial viability.

ISBN 1-56327-007-2 / 1344 pages / $90.00 / Order HPM-B261

Productivity Press, Inc., Dept. BK, P.O. Box 13390, Portland, OR 97213-0390
Telephone: 1-800-394-6868   Fax: 1-800-394-6286

The Hunters and the Hunted
A Non-Linear Solution for Reengineering the Workplace
James B. Swartz

Our competitive environment changes rapidly. If you want to survive, you have to stay on top of those changes. Otherwise, you become prey to your competitors. Hunters continuously change and learn; anyone who doesn't becomes the hunted and sooner or later will be devoured. This unusual non-fiction novel provides a veritable crash course in continuous transformation. It offers lessons from real-life companies and introduces many industrial gurus as characters. *The Hunters and the Hunted* doesn't simply tell you how to change; it puts you inside the change process itself.

ISBN 1-56327-043-9 / 582 pages / $45.00 / Order HUNT-B261

Implementing a Lean Management System
Thomas L. Jackson with Constance E. Dyer

Does your company think and act ahead of technological change, ahead of the customer, and ahead of the competition? Thinking strategically requires a company to face these questions with a clear future image of itself. *Implementing a Lean Management System* lays out a comprehensive management system for aligning the firm's vision of the future with market realities. Based on hoshin management, the Japanese strategic planning method used by top managers for driving TQM throughout an organization, Lean Management is about deploying vision, strategy, and policy to all levels of daily activity. It is an eminently practical methodology emerging out of the implementation of continuous improvement methods and employee involvement. The key tools of this book build on the knowledge of the worker, multi-skilling, and an understanding of the role and responsibilities of the new lean manufacturer.

ISBN 1-56327-085-4 / est. 150 pages / $65.00 / Order ILMS-B261

Productivity Press, Inc., Dept. BK, P.O. Box 13390, Portland, OR 97213-0390
Telephone: 1-800-394-6868   Fax: 1-800-394-6286

Corporate Diagnosis
Meeting Global Standards for Excellence
Thomas L. Jackson with Constance E. Dyer

All too often, strategic planning neglects an essential first step-and final step-diagnosis of the organization's current state. What's required is a systematic review of the critical factors in organizational learning and growth, factors that require monitoring, measurement, and management to ensure that your company competes successfully. This executive workbook provides a step-by-step method for diagnosing an organization's strategic health and measuring its overall competitiveness against world class standards. With checklists, charts, and detailed explanations, *Corporate Diagnosis* is a practical instruction manual. The pillars of Jackson's diagnostic system are strategy, structure, and capability. Detailed diagnostic questions in each area are provided as guidelines for developing your own self-assessment survey.

ISBN 1-56327-086-2 / est. 100 pages / $65.00 / Order CDIAG-B261

Integrated Cost Management
A Companywide Prescription for Higher Profits and Lower Costs
Michiharu Sakurai

To survive and grow, leading-edge companies around the world recognize the need for new management accounting systems suited for today's advanced manufacturing technology. Accountants must become interdisciplinary to cope with increasing cross-functionality, flexibility, and responsiveness. This book provides an analysis of current best practices in management accounting in the U.S. and Japan. It covers critical issues and specific methods related to factory automation and computer integrated manufacturing (CIM), including target costing, overhead management, activity-based management (ABM), and the cost management of software development. Sakurai's brilliant analysis lays the foundation for a more sophisticated understanding of the true value that management accounting holds in every aspect of your company.

ISBN 1-56327-054-4 / 319 pages / $50.00 / Order ICM-B261

Productivity Press, Inc., Dept. BK, P.O. Box 13390, Portland, OR 97213-0390
Telephone: 1-800-394-6868   Fax: 1-800-394-6286

Manufacturing Strategy
How to Formulate and Implement a Winning Plan
John Miltenburg

This book offers a step-by-step method for creating a strategic manufacturing plan. The key tool is a multidimensional worksheet that links the competitive analysis to manufacturing outputs, the seven basic production systems, the levels of capability and the levers for moving to a higher level. The author presents each element of the worksheet and shows you how to link them to create an integrated strategy and implementation plan. By identifying the appropriate production system for your business, you can determine what output you can expect from manufacturing, how to improve outputs, and how to change to more optimal production systems as your business needs changes. This is a valuable book for general managers, operations managers, engineering managers, marketing managers, comptrollers, consultants, and corporate staff in any manufacturing company

ISBN 1-56327-071-4 / 391 pages / $45.00 / Order MANST-B261

A New American TQM
Four Practical Revolutions in Management
Shoji Shiba, Alan Graham, and David Walden

For TQM to succeed in America, you need to create an American-style "learning organization" with the full commitment and understanding of senior managers and executives. Written expressly for this audience, *A New American TQM* offers a comprehensive and detailed explanation of TQM and how to implement it, based on courses taught at MIT's Sloan School of Management and the Center for Quality Management, a consortium of American companies. Full of case studies and amply illustrated, the book examines major quality tools and how they are being used by the most progressive American companies today.

ISBN 1-56327-032-3 / 606 pages / $50.00 / Order NATQM-B261

Productivity Press, Inc., Dept. BK, P.O. Box 13390, Portland, OR 97213-0390
Telephone: 1-800-394-6868   Fax: 1-800-394-6286

Performance Measurement for World Class Manufacturing
A Model for American Companies
Brian H. Maskell

If your company is adopting world class manufacturing techniques, you'll need new methods of performance measurement to control production variables. In practical terms, this book describes the new methods of performance measurement and how they are used in a changing environment. For manufacturing managers as well as cost accountants, it provides a theoretical foundation of these innovative methods supported by extensive practical examples. The book specifically addresses performance measures for delivery, process time, production flexibility, quality, and finance.

ISBN 0-915299-99-2 / 448 pages / $55.00 / Order PERFM-B261

Today and Tomorrow
Henry Ford

This autobiography by the world's most famous automaker reveals the thinking that changed industry forever, and provided the inspiration for just-in-time. Today these ideas are re-emerging to revitalize American industry. Here's the man who doubled wages, cut the price of a car in half, and produced over 2 million units a year. You will be enlightened and intrigued by the words of this colorful and remarkable man.

ISBN 0-915299-36-4 / 300 pages / $30.00 / Order FORD-B261

The Unshackled Organization
Facing the Challenge of Unpredictability Through Spontaneous Reorganization
Jeffrey Goldstein

Managers should not necessarily try to solve all the internal problems within their organizations; intervention may help in the short term, but in the long run may inhibit true problem-solving change from taking place. And change is the real goal. Through change comes real hope for improvement. Using leading-edge scientific and social theories about change, Goldstein explores how change happens within an organization and reveals that only through "self-organization" can natural, lasting change occur. This book is a pragmatic guide for managers, executives, consultants, and other change agents.

ISBN 1-56327-048-X / 208 pages / $25.00 / Order UO-B261

Productivity Press, Inc., Dept. BK, P.O. Box 13390, Portland, OR 97213-0390
Telephone: 1-800-394-6868   Fax: 1-800-394-6286

Management Alert: Don't Reform—Transform!

Michael J. Kami

In today's fast-changing world, CEO's and their executive teams must change their ways, adapt faster, act differently, and perform better. And managers and employees at all levels must also undergo a revolution through new organization, better training, and broader empowerment. In *Management Alert: Don't Reform—Transform*, Michael Kami describes the needed changes, and how they can be achieved throughout the company.

ISBN 1-56327-064-1 / 53 pages / $15.95 / Order MS1-B261

16 Point Strategy for Productivity and Total Quality Control

William F. Christopher and Carl G. Thor

Major breakthroughs in productivity improvement can only be achieved when one is willing to make major changes. This book provides the definitive list of what must be considered when implementing continuous improvement methods throughout an organization.

ISBN 1-56327-072-2 / 69 pages / $15.95 / Order Item # MS7-B261

New Performance Measures

Brian H. Maskell

Traditional performance measurements are not only ineffective for today's world class organizations, they can actually be harmful — they measure the wrong things. World class companies need measurements that can help them in their quest for improvement. You have to start measuring what your customers really care about such as customer service, quality, and flexibility. Implementing new continuous improvement programs while still using traditional performance measurements will only set you back and give you a lot of useless data. In *New Performance Measures*, you'll learn how to start measuring the things you truly need to know.

ISBN 1-56327-063-3 / 58 pages / $15.95 / Order MS4-B261

Productivity Press, Inc., Dept. BK, P.O. Box 13390, Portland, OR 97213-0390
Telephone: 1-800-394-6868   Fax: 1-800-394-6286

TO ORDER: Write, phone, or fax Productivity Press, Dept. BK, P.O. Box 13390, Portland, OR 97213-0390, phone 1-800-394-6868, fax 1-800-394-6286. Send check or charge to your credit card (American Express, Visa, MasterCard accepted).

U.S. ORDERS; Add $5 shipping for first book, $2 each additional for UPS surface delivery. Add $5 for each AV program containing 1 or 2 tapes; add $12 for each AV program containing 3 or more tapes. We offer attractive quantity discounts for bulk purchases of individual titles; call for more information.

ORDER BY E-MAIL: Order 24 hours a day from anywhere in the world. Use either address:

To order: *service@ppress.com*

To view the online catalog and/or order: *http://www.ppress.com/*

QUANTITY DISCOUNTS: For information on quantity discounts, please contact our sales department.

INTERNATIONAL ORDERS: Write, phone, or fax for quote and indicate shipping method desired. For international callers, telephone number is 503-235-0600 and fax number is 503-235-0909. Prepayment in U.S. dollars must accompany your order (checks must be drawn on U.S. banks). When quote is returned with payment, your order will be shipped promptly by the method requested.

NOTE: *Prices are in U.S. dollars and are subject to change without notice.*